JENKINS OF GREENBOTTOM

A Civil War Saga

JENKINS OF GREENBOTTOM

A Civil War Saga

by Jack L. Dickinson

The oil painting of Albert G. Jenkins completed in 1937 by the Works Progress Administration (WPA) for the dedication of the Jenkins Training School.
Courtesy: Morrow Library, Marshall University

PICTORIAL HISTORIES PUBLISHING COMPANY

Charleston, West Virginia 25304

LIBRARY OF CONGRESS
CATALOG CARD NUMBER 88-68494

ISBN 0-933126-95-6

First Printing: April 1988

Typography: Arrow Graphics
Layout: Stan Cohen
Cover Painting: Jeffrey Dickinson

PICTORIAL HISTORIES PUBLISHING COMPANY
4103 Virginia Ave. S.E.
Charleston, West Virginia 25304

FOREWORD

"Albert G. Jenkins . . . is a spectator-spy;
a fire-eating slaveholder. . . ."
ELI THAYER
CEREDO, VA., 1857

"Living as they do upon the border of a border
state and having scarcely enough of the
institution of slavery in their midst to justify the
name . . . it will be an inviting point of attack
on the part of northern fanaticism. . . ."
ALBERT G. JENKINS
FEB. 28, 1860

Brig. Gen. Albert Gallatin Jenkins:
". . . he is no doubt a gallant officer & true
patriot but judging from his Brigade he is not a
good disciplinarian & I recommend its (his
resignation) acceptance in order that a good
disciplinarian & experienced Cav officer may
mould the best material I know of into
a fine cavalry Brigade."
J.E.B. STUART
AUG. 5, 1863

". . . I can not recommend the acceptance of his
resignation. He is a gallant officer, has
organized a large brigade of brave men who only
require instruction. I know of no one now
with whom to replace him."
R. E. LEE
8TH AUG. 1863

". . . A great general is merely a great
psychologist—with a trace of the Indian
in his make-up."
ALBERT G. JENKINS (II)
APRIL 2, 1938

ACKNOWLEDGMENT

I wish to give special thanks to certain people who made contributions to this work. My wife, Kay, who acted as research assistant and editor deserves special thanks for her special patience. Jane Wallace of Huntington loaned us several original photographs and other material from George S. Wallace's collection that exist nowhere else. Terry Lowry, noted West Virginia Civil War historian, also contributed photos and information. Cora Teel of the James E. Morrow Library at Marshall University loaned original letters and documents from the Jenkins family, and assisted with other research. Bill Wintz of the Upper Vandalia Historical Society loaned the Victoria Hansford Teays diaries and other historical information on the Kanawha Valley. Jeff Guinn of Vermont loaned photos of the Jenkins sword. Mark Meadows of Camp Garnett, Sons of Confederate Veterans, donated photos of Greenbottom.

DEDICATED TO THE CONFEDERATE SOLDIER OF WESTERN VIRGINIA AND HIS DESCENDANTS.

Grave of Albert G. Jenkins in the Confederate plot in Spring Hill Cemetery, Huntington, W.Va. This headstone was moved along with his remains from the family plot at Greenbottom in Dec. of 1891.
Author's collection

TABLE OF CONTENTS

State historical marker that stood at Greenbottom. It was stolen in the 1970s and has not been replaced.

CHAPTER ONE

Virginia Valley Background

Throughout the history of Virginia and West Virginia, the "Virginia Valley" has served as the funnel through which many families have passed on their migration west of the Allegheny Mountains. In the early to middle 1700s several attempts were made to move west of the Alleghenies, but the Indians continued to mount attacks against the pioneers, until finally some settlements were strong enough to survive.

It is, therefore, not surprising that the Jenkins family has roots in the Valley, and in Rockbridge County, Va., in particular.

Before we discuss the early history of the Jenkins family, let us examine the family of William A. Jenkins' bride, Jeannette Grigsby McNutt. Her father, Alexander McNutt, was a soldier in the Revolution, holding the rank of ensign in the Rockbridge Militia as late as 1781. He was born about the year 1756, probably the son of John McNutt and Catherine Anderson. He married Rachael Grigsby, daughter of John and Elizabeth Grigsby, who was born about 1771. They were married Jan. 7, 1790, in Rockbridge County and made their home near the present site of Buena Vista on the North River in that county. Both died there and are buried in the Stonewall Jackson Cemetery at Lexington, Va. Their large monument reads: "A tribute, by his daughter, Sarah Sims of Vicksburg, Miss., to the memory of Alexander McNutt, who died March 29, 1812, aged 56 years." On the reverse is a similar inscription: "to Rachel McNutt, who died Jan. 7, 1840, aged 69." Alexander McNutt and Rachael had at least nine children, as follows:

1. Sarah, who married a Sims and lived in Vicksburg.
2. Alexander G., who never married and died in Rockbridge County in 1848. He was educated at Washington College and was a lawyer at Jackson, Miss. He was also elected governor of Mississippi.
3. Jeannette, who was born on Sept. 19, 1803, in Rockbridge County, and married William Jenkins on Oct. 5, 1824, in Rockbridge. She died April 29, 1843, at Greenbottom, Cabell County, Va. (now West Virginia). She is buried in Spring Hill Cemetery, Huntington, WVa.
4. Joseph.
5. Anderson.
6. Benjamin.
7. John, who died before 1834.
8. Catharine.
9. Gallatin.

William A. Jenkins, known as "Captain Jenkins," was the son of Eustace Lacy Jenkins. Eustace Lacy Jenkins does not appear in any census records as the head of the Jenkins family. Since the first actual United States census was conducted in 1790, it is possible that he was deceased by that time. It is also possible, however, that he is the same Eustace Jenkins shown as "Eustacey" Jenkins in the military records of the War of 1812. This Jenkins was a private in Captain Burrows' Company of Sea Fencibles from New York. We have only found records of two children of Eustace Lacy Jenkins, who are:

1. William A.: born about 1777, and died Nov. 17, 1859, on his plantation or large farm at Greenbottom, Cabell Co. We do not know if William A. Jenkins was actually born in Rockbridge County, or elsewhere in Virginia. He is buried with his wife, Jeannette, in Spring Hill Cemetery in Huntington, W.Va. Both were originally buried in the family cemetery at Greenbottom, but their bodies were moved to Spring Hill in 1940. The large monument marking their graves was also moved by wagon, at the same time.

2. Eustatia J.: born about 1806, and came with her brother William to Cabell County in 1825. She married David R. Lacy, who was born in Virginia about 1797. They were married on Dec. 2, 1834, in Cabell County. They lived near the Jenkins mansion at Greenbottom. She was also originally buried at Greenbottom. Her body was moved to Spring Hill Cemetery in 1940. Her headstone reads simply: "Eustatia Jenkins Lacy, died at an advanced age in 1873." David R. Lacy was a brickmason in Cabell County, and died after 1870. David and Eustatia had at least two children, both boys. Both were born in Cabell County in the 1830s.

CHAPTER TWO

CAPT. WILLIAM JENKINS AND THE GREENBOTTOM PLANTATION

WILLIAM A. JENKINS, SON OF EUSTACE LACY JENKINS, WAS BORN IN 1777 in Virginia. By the time he was in his thirties, William Jenkins had built up a substantial business in Tidewater, Va., where he operated a shipping line. He began by running small boats up the James River to Lynchburg carrying tobacco, grain and livestock. He then expanded his operation by exporting wheat from Norfolk, Va., to ports on the coast of Brazil. These ships brought back cargoes of coffee on their return trips. It is from this occupation that William probably gained his nickname of "Captain." William Jenkins served in the War of 1812, but only as a private.

William then moved to Rockbridge County in the Virginia Valley. He was probably living there before 1817. On Feb. 8 of that year William purchased a portion of land on the north fork of the James River. He bought an adjoining tract of land on June 25, 1819. He met Jeannette Grigsby McNutt of Rockbridge and they were married on Oct. 5, 1824. The large farm that William Jenkins and Jeannette built up in Rockbridge County was known as "Buffalo Forge." Their first child, Eustatia, was born there on Sept. 3, 1825.

According to various sources, William, Jeannette and Eustatia moved to Cabell County, Va. (now West Virginia), when little Eustatia was only three weeks old. Also traveling with them was William's sister, Eustatia J. Upon arriving in Cabell, William purchased 4,395 acres of the Greenbottom lands from John Coalter and John Cocke, trustees of Gov. William H. Cabell. This deed was dated Sept. 20, 1825. The price in notes and cash was $15,000.

The Greenbottom lands are located just north of the famous Savage Grant in Cabell County. The first settler in that area was probably either Wilson C. Nicholas or a Mr. Spurlock. Spurlock was living on the Greenbottom lands in March of 1805.

On Oct. 30, 1826, William and Jeannette Jenkins sold their 334 acres of land in Rockbridge County to William Paxton.

William Jenkins erected a temporary wooden house on the Greenbottom property, while he was building his large brick mansion house. This wooden house stood between the present home and Route 2, close to the B & O Railway tracks. He began farming the estate and by the time of the 1830 census of Cabell County, had 33 slaves working the fields of grain and corn. This had risen to 37 slaves by 1840. The slaves who died on the plantation were supposedly buried in one of the cornfields on the northern end of the property. Some of the older residents of the area stated that this was close to the Mason County line, near what was then the Clover Post Office.

William's three sons were born in the temporary house. Thomas Jefferson was born there on Nov. 22, 1826. William Alexander was born there on Nov. 21, 1828,

Map of Cabell County, W.Va., published in 1884. The Greenbottom area is at the top of the map, in the bend of the Ohio River.

Albert Gallatin was born there on Nov. 10, 1830.

The bricks used in the permanent house were baked from the clay dug from the river bank at a temporary brick factory on the estate. The wood and timbers were cut from the forest a short distance away from the Ohio River. The brick house was completed in 1835. The house still stands today, a monument to its sturdy construction. This house at Greenbottom is known as the "Homestead." A large brick kitchen and wooden slave house were built separate from the mansion house, as was the custom of that period. The front of the house faces the Ohio River, and a road was cut down to a landing at the riverbank, where the steamboats regularly stopped. Here the Jenkins workers loaded the products of the plantation on the boats to be transported downriver.

In the late 1840s, Captain Jenkins built a law office near the mansion for use by his son, Albert G. Jenkins. This law office stood on a stone slab just to the south of the main house. This stone slab is still visible today. After the initial arrangements were made, William Jenkins went on a trip of some duration, leaving Albert to supervise the completion of the construction. Upon the return of William Jenkins, he found that young Albert had failed to have the stones finished on both sides, evidently feeling that the finish on the outside was sufficient. The Captain disagreed, and had the workmen pull down the wall that had been built and had the stones finished on both sides. When this was done, the office was finally completed as planned. The law office, brick kitchen, and slave house were destroyed during the Ohio River flood of 1913.

By the 1850 census of Virginia, the Jenkins real estate was shown as having a value of $80,000. This estimate made the Jenkins estate the most valuable farm or plantation in Cabell County.

To give an indication of the scale of the production of the Jenkins estate, in 1861 when Union soldiers raided the Jenkins plantation, they found 10,000 bushels of corn already harvested. They also confiscated 16 "fat cattle," four horses, and two mules.

William sent all four of his children to college. His three sons were all scheduled so they attended together, going by steamboat to Jefferson College in Pennsylvania in 1848.

Jeannette G. Jenkins died on April 29, 1843, of consumption and was buried in the family cemetery at Greenbottom. William Jenkins contracted pneumonia, died on Nov. 17, 1859, and was buried beside his wife at Greenbottom. Captain Jenkins was buried in a cast iron vault. Both William and Jeannette were reinterred in Spring Hill Cemetery at Huntington in 1940, due to the efforts of their daughter Margaret Virginia. When the graves were moved, a mule with heavy chains was required to pull the cast iron casket out of the ground and to move the 10-foot-high monument that stood over the graves of William and Jeannette Jenkins.

In his will, William Jenkins divided his plantation equally among his three sons. In addition, he bequeathed his house and lot in Lynchburg, Va., and $50,000 in currency or bonds to his daughter, Eustatia Waugh. He also bequeathed to his sister a slave, Mary, and her issue. He ordered his slave Jacob to be sold to one of his three sons, whichever was the highest bidder. He also left the sum of $5,000 in trust to pay a minister of the gospel to preach ". . . in a church in Green Bottom which it is my intention to erect. . . ." William Jenkins added the unusual clause to his will that if any of the legatees contested the will, that person would receive nothing under the will, and his portion would be divided among the remaining legatees. Albert Gallatin received the

Earliest known photo of the Jenkins mansion at Greenbottom. It appears much as it did during the Civil War. Circa 1880-1890. George S. Wallace Collection, courtesy Jane Wallace

The Jenkins mansion at Greenbottom about the turn of the century, before the addition of the wooden section. George S. Wallace Collection, courtesy Jane Wallace

uppermost tract, which included the mansion house. Thomas Jefferson received the middle tract, and he constructed his house on that portion. William Alexander received the southernmost tract, and constructed a brick mansion on that portion.

The Homestead at Greenbottom has been continuously occupied since its completion. Margaret Virginia Jenkins attempted to convey the home in 1929 to the local chapter of the United Daughters of the Confederacy. They were to restore it and maintain it as a memorial. Due to the estate dispute, discussed in detail in a later chapter, the property was never transferred. The house has been occupied in the last several years by James and Carla Knight. The home was placed on the National Register of Historic Places in 1978.

Frederic A. Macdonald, who lived in the house with his parents about 1910, related a legend about "the ghost of General Jenkins." Supposedly, while at Harvard Albert Gallatin Jenkins acquired some skill at ten-pin bowling. Before the Civil War, Jenkins was supposed to have built a bowling alley in the attic of the house. Macdonald related a story of the ghost returning to the Homestead to bowl a solitary game of tenpins in the attic. He finally explained that his father proved that squirrels dropping acorns and nuts in an opening beside the chimney was the explanation for the "ghost."

The mansion at Greenbottom as it appears today. Albert G. Jenkins' small law office stood just to the right of the chimney. Author's collection

WILL OF WILLIAM JENKINS
Cabell County Wills, Book 2, p. 343

In the name of God, Amen.

Being of sound mind, but feeling the bodily infirmities of age, and being moreover desirous of arranging all my affairs connected with this world in order that I may leave a proper and undisturbed contemplation of that future state which awaits us all, and that further feeling a natural parental solicitude to establish and regulate beyond the possibility of dispute or contention the interest of my children as appurtaining to my property—therefore, I Wm Jenkins of Green Bottom, Cabell County Va do make publish and declare this to be my last Will & Testament as follows.

I give and bequeath my estate known as Green Bottom to my three sons, Thomas J. Jenkins, Wm A. Jenkins & Albert G. Jenkins to have & to hold the same seperately & singly in fee simple according to the following apportionment & division, that is to say I give & bequeath to my son Albert G. Jenkins in fee simple (subject to a life estate in a small lot in favour of my sister Eustatia Lacy to be mentioned hereafter) all that part of Green Bottom (including also the tract since bought by me known as the Goff place) lying above the following line. To wit, a line commencing at a stone set in the ground which I shall have marked No.1 about fifteen feet south west from the centre of an old site known as "Britain's House." Thence running due north sixty poles to a large sycamore on the bank of the Ohio River, thence due north as far into the Ohio River as the estate of Green Bottom lawfully extends then going back to the stone before mentioned. Thence S18 (degrees) E106 poles to another stone set in the ground thence S6 (degrees) E to another stone set in the ground 9 poles west of Chases Spring, thence S12 (degrees) E 470 1/4 poles to two white oaks on the bank of a hill in the back line of Green Bottom.

To my son Thomas J. Jenkins I give & bequeath in fee simple all that portion of Green Bottom lying between the above described line of Albert G. Jenkins and another line described as follows. Beginning at the back line of Green Bottom at a stone set in the ground in a field near the foot of a hill, thence N70 (degrees) W513 poles to a stone set in the ground at the north side of an elm tree thence N76 (degrees) W158 1/2 poles to a stone set in the ground to be marked No.2. Thence W2 1/2 poles to a buck tree on the bank of the river thence west as far into the Ohio River as the estate of Green Bottom lawfully extends. To my son Wm A. Jenkins I give and bequeath in fee simple all that part of Green Bottom lying below the last described line; the words above and below as herein used having reference to the course of the Ohio River. I also further give & bequeath to each of my sons Thos. J. Jenkins, Wm A. Jenkins & Albert G. Jenkins, the slaves, horses, mules hogs & stock of every description of which I have already put them in possession, together with all increase which may hereafter spring from the same, the legal seizure or fee, however both of all such stock as well as of the land aforesaid to remain in —?— until my death. To my daughter Eustatia A. Waugh I give & bequeath my house and lot in Lynchburg, Va No. 38 Main St. S side and fifty Thousand ($50,000) in currency or bonds according to the form in which the same may be found at the time of my death. To my sister Eustatia Lacy I bequeath a life estate in the lot of land upon which she now resides (remainder in fee simple to my son Albert G. Jenkins). My slave Mary & her issue I bequeath to my sister before mentioned for the

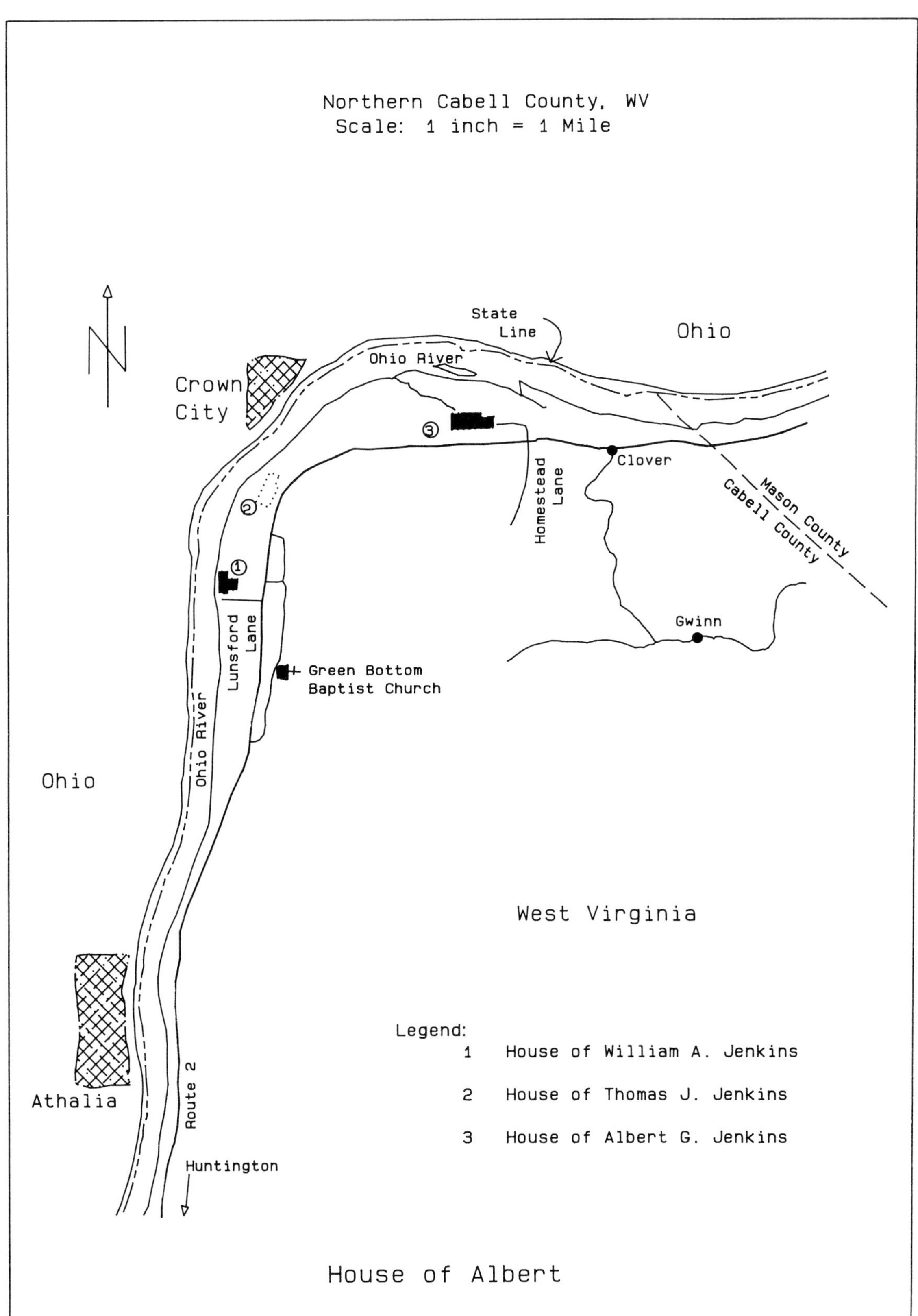

Map of northern Cabell County, W.Va., showing locations of the three Jenkins mansions.

time of her natural life. My slave Jacob I will to be sold to whomsoever of my three sons will pay the highest price for him—and also the slave Mary & her issue to be similarly disposed of at the death of my sister aforesaid and this sum to be increased by an addition from my property or money not already disposed of, until it reaches the sum of five thousand. Said sum of five thousand dollars to be given to my three sons in trust for the following purposes to put the same out at interest & to apply the interest thereto according to the payment of such minister of the gospel as they procure to preach in a church in Green Bottom which it is my intention to erect if God spares life & breath for me so to do; if I am not spared to build said church it is my will that the sum of (blank) dollars shall be taken from my money or property not already disposed of and applied to the building of said church on some suitable spot on Green Bottom, by my executors, it is my further will that from the residue of my property or money all my debts shall be paid if any I owe and then five thousand dollars be given to my son Thomas J. Jenkins and after that time all the residue of whatever description be equally divided between my three sons before mentioned. It is my further will that should any of the legatees of this instrument or any other person at this instance attempts to set aside the same, then such legatees shall take nothing under this will but the portion granted them shall be divided equally between the other legatees. I appoint as my executors of this testament my three sons before mentioned. In witness thereof I have hereunto subscribed my name & affixed my seal on this A.D. 1857.

Wm Jenkins (seal)

Witnessed by . . . with their respective places of residence:

R. A. Richardson	Cabell Co. Va
Eastham H. Hausen	Mason Co. Va
H. B. Strus	Cabell Co. Va

Base of the Jenkins family monument in Spring Hill. It stands over the graves of Capt. William Jenkins and his wife Jeannette.
Author's collection

Footstones of William and Jeannette Jenkins in Spring Hill Cemetery.
Author's collection

The Jenkins family monument in Spring Hill Cemetery, Huntington, WVa. It was moved from the family cemetery at Greenbottom in 1940.
Author's collection

CHAPTER THREE

EUSTACIA A. JENKINS

EUSTACIA JENKINS, FIRST CHILD OF WILLIAM JENKINS AND JEANNETTE Grigsby McNutt, was born Sept. 3, 1825. She was born in Rockbridge County, Va., when William and Jeannette still lived at Buffalo Forge. She was named for William's father, Eustace Lacy Jenkins. She came with her father and mother to Cabell County when only three weeks old. After finishing her early schooling, she was supposedly one of the first females to receive a scholarship to Oberlin College in Ohio, and was rumored to have attended there in the 1840s. Oberlin College, however, has no record of her attendance. Oberlin, in fact, was known as an abolitionist, anti-slavery school which had Negro students in its student body. It, therefore, seems very unlikely that a prominent Southern family would send their daughter to this Northern abolitionist college.

Eustacia married Pembroke Waugh of Lynchburg, Va. He was born about 1817-18, probably the son of Nicholas Waugh of Amherst County. They were living in Amherst County by the time of the 1850 census. Their real estate was valued in that census as $30,000. In his will, her father, William Jenkins, left to Eustacia his house and lot at No. 38 Main Street, south side, in Lynchburg and $50,000 in currency or bonds. (Amherst County borders Lynchburg on the north side.) By the 1860 census, when Eustacia had inherited her estate from her father, Pembroke's real estate was valued at $20,000 and his personal property was valued at $15,000. Eustacia's real estate was valued at $5,000 and her personal property was valued at $35,000. The 1860 slave schedules showed that they owned 101 slaves. Eustacia does not appear in the 1870 census with Pembroke Waugh and family. It is possible she died between 1863 and 1870.

At least six children were born to this marriage, as follows:

1. Isabella, born about 1848. She married a Mr. Woods. She was living at Pedlar Mills, Amherst Co., Va., in 1915.
2. William M., born about 1853.
3. J. V. (male), born about 1855 and possibly died before 1870.
4. Albert Gallatin, born about 1858.
5. Virginia, born about 1860 and possibly died before 1870.
6. Ashby, born about 1863 and probably named for Confederate General Turner Ashby.

Ruins of the Thomas J. Jenkins house, which stood between the houses of his two brothers on the Greenbottom lands. The house burned about 1925.
Author's collection

CHAPTER FOUR

THOMAS JEFFERSON JENKINS

THOMAS JEFFERSON JENKINS, SECOND CHILD OF WILLIAM JENKINS AND Jeannette Grigsby McNutt was born on Nov. 22, 1826, at Greenbottom, Cabell County, Va. He was born in the temporary wood house built before the brick mansion was completed. After his education as a youth, probably by private tutor, he went along with his two brothers to Jefferson College in Pennsylvania. He graduated from there in 1848.

Thomas J. Jenkins married first Arianna Buffington, daughter of Maj. James Buffington. Arianna was born about 1831 in Virginia before the Buffingtons moved to Ohio. They were married on Jan. 16, 1851, in Lawrence Co., Ohio. James, her father, was the son of Thomas Buffington, who moved onto the Savage Grant in Cabell County near Guyandotte in the late 1700s. Major James Buffington and his family moved to Lawrence County soon after Arianna was born. Thomas Jenkins was partners in Thomas Buffington and Company which built a large grist mill in Guyandotte. This company even had its own steamboat, named the "Dr. Buffington." Most of Guyandotte, along with the grist mill, was burned by Union troops on Nov. 11, 1861, following the Confederate attack and capture of Union recruits. Arianna died on Sept. 15, 1851, at the home of her father near Quaker Bottom, Ohio.

On Nov. 18, 1856, Thomas married in Cabell County Susan L. Holderby, daughter of Robert Holderby and Susan Ann Chapman. She was born in 1836 in Cabell County.

Upon the death of his father, Thomas Jefferson inherited the middle third of the Greenbottom estate. This amounted to 1,465 acres. On this portion, he erected a fine home and farmed his land. This house stood close to the present-day Route 2 and was midway between the mansions of his two brothers. The house burned in the 1920s. In the 1860 census of Virginia, Thomas's portion of real estate was valued at $90,000 and his personal property at $10,000.

Thomas J. Jenkins enlisted with his brothers in the Border Rangers, which became Company E of the 8th Virginia Cavalry, Confederate States Army. He enlisted on May 29, 1861, at Greenbottom. This was the date when his brother, Albert G. Jenkins, organized the company. Postwar sources state that Thomas was promoted to major in 1863, but there are no official records to support this. There is a voucher in his file dated December 1862 that could have "major" in front of his name, but the ink is smeared. After the Civil War he and other ex-Confederates were defendants in several law suits over the supposed destruction of property during the war, and several people did manage to attach parts of their estates.

Thomas J. Jenkins died on Aug. 1, 1872, in Cabell County of heart disease supposedly caused by "military exposure" during the war. He is buried in the Holderby plot in Spring Hill Cemetery in Huntington, W.Va. Susan Holderby Jenkins died in

1927 and is also buried in Spring Hill. Thomas J. and Susan had six children, as follows:

1. Julia Holderby: born in 1857 in Cabell County, and died in 1908. She never married and is also buried in Spring Hill Cemetery.

2. Laura P.: born on Aug. 25, 1859, in Cabell County, and died on May 11, 1879. She never married and is also buried in Spring Hill.

3. Dudley J.: born in 1861, married Elizabeth Leete of Ironton, Ohio. He attempted to get into the oil and gas business by drilling a dry hole on the Jenkins farm about 1895. D. J. was sheriff of Cabell County from 1893 to 1896. He was elected on Nov. 8, 1892, to serve for four years. His mother was one of the sureties for his sheriff's bond. He was still living in Ohio in 1910.

4. Ada Grace: born in Cabell County on Feb. 21, 1866. She lived with her mother in New York in 1910. She was living at 211 South 8th Street, Ironton, Ohio, in 1938. She attended the ceremony dedicating the Jenkins Training School at Marshall College on April 6, 1938.

5. George Robert: Born in Cabell County in late 1872 or early 1873. Became a dentist in New York City. He lived at 2 East 54th Street in 1938. He attended the dedication of the Jenkins Training School at Marshall College on April 6, 1938, and in 1961 was living in Bethesda, Md.

6. Albert Gallatin: born in Cabell County on Jan. 14, 1872. He served in WWI as a private in the quartermaster corps. He was living with his sister Grace at 211 South 8th Street, Ironton, Ohio, in 1938. He entered the Huntington Veteran's Hospital in that year for the removal of cataracts. He died April 3, 1957, and is also buried in Spring Hill Cemetery.

Guests and officials present at the opening of the Albert Gallatin Jenkins Training School at Marshall College, April 6, 1938. Grace Jenkins is 3rd from right in the front row. Dr. George R. Jenkins is 4th from right. Col. George S. Wallace, author of *Cabell Annals and Families*, is in the 2nd row, 3rd from left. Courtesy: Morrow Library, Marshall University

CHAPTER FIVE

DR. WILLIAM ALEXANDER JENKINS

WILLIAM ALEXANDER JENKINS, THIRD CHILD OF WILLIAM JENKINS and Jeannette McNutt, was born Nov. 21, 1828 at Greenbottom, Cabell Co., Va. He was also born in the wooden house before his father's brick mansion was completed. After his education as a youth, probably by private tutor, he attended Jefferson College in Pennsylvania with his two brothers. He also graduated from there in 1848. He then went on to attend Jefferson Medical College in Philadelphia, which was a branch of Jefferson College. He might have practiced medicine at Greenbottom for a short time as he is found in the 1850 census of Cabell County, living with his father and listed as physician.

William A. practiced medicine in St. Louis, Mo., from 1852 to 1854. While there he met and married Julia M. Reed. She was born Jan. 13, 1829, in St. Louis. They were married on Dec. 22, 1853, in St. Louis.

William A. inherited one-third of the Greenbottom estate at the death of his father in 1859. His portion amounted to 1,465 acres. On his portion William Alexander erected a two-story brick house, which still stands at the end of Lunsford Lane. The house stands opposite Crown City, Ohio. Beautiful decorations adorned the ceilings and trim in all the rooms. This trim (existing now in only one downstairs room) consists of acorns and branches of oak trees. William's house was larger and more expensively decorated when originally built than the mansion erected by his father. In the 1860 census of Cabell County, William A.'s real estate was valued at $80,000 and his personal property at $15,000.

Postwar sources agree that William A. was a surgeon with the 8th Virginia Cavalry, Confederate States Army, during the Civil War. Both of his brothers were in the 8th Virginia Cavalry. He does not appear in the official records. Perhaps rather than formally enlisting, he merely accompanied the regiment as one of the surgeons.

William A. died on April 18, 1877 in St. Louis of paresis of the brain and is buried in Spring Hill Cemetery, Huntington, W.Va. Julia M., his wife, died on Nov. 19, 1894. She, too, is buried in Spring Hill. William and Julia had six children, as follows:

1. Jeannette A.: born 1854 in Cabell County, and married Samuel L. Butler. He was born in 1851 in Giles Co., Va. They were married on Oct. 2, 1879, in Cabell County. She died in 1912 and is buried in Spring Hill Cemetery.

2. William G.: born 1857, no further data.

3. Charles B. McNutt: born in 1858 and died Oct. 24, 1859, of dysentery. He was originally buried in the family cemetery at Greenbottom, but his body was moved in 1940 to Spring Hill.

4. Kenrick A.: born in 1861, and died on Sept. 1, 1868, of fever. He is buried in Spring Hill, where his headstone gives his name as Kenrick A. Cabell County death records list his name as Augustus K.

5. Julia M.: born ca. 1863.

6. Susan M.: born in 1863, and married C.E. Gwinn. They lived at 1240 Bryden Road, Columbus, Ohio, in the 1930s. She died in 1935.

Early view of the Dr. William A. Jenkins home. From a painting when the house was first built, about 1860. The boxwoods in front of the porch had recently been planted. George S. Wallace Collection, courtesy Jane Wallace

Another view of the Dr. William A. Jenkins home. Photo circa 1910. The boxwoods in front of the porch are much larger. George S. Wallace Collection, courtesy Jane Wallace

Another view of the Dr. William A. Jenkins home as it appears today. The boxwoods are now claimed to be the largest in Cabell County. Author's collection

Photo of the interior of the Dr. William A. Jenkins home, showing the detail of the ceiling design. All the rooms in the house were decorated with this type of detailing. Only this piece remains. Author's collection

Marshall Academy as it appeared when the Jenkins brothers attended there in 1845. This brick building was completed in 1839 to replace the log structure which served as both a church and the school. (Now the site of Marshall University in Huntington, WVa.)
Sketch by Jeff Dickinson

CHAPTER SIX

ALBERT GALLATIN JENKINS

EARLY CHILDHOOD: 1830-1845

ALBERT GALLATIN JENKINS, FOURTH AND LAST CHILD OF WILLIAM Jenkins and Jeannette Grigsby McNutt, was born on Nov. 10, 1830. He was named for Albert Gallatin, U. S. Senator in 1793, who was Thomas Jefferson's secretary of the treasury. He, like his brothers, was also born in the temporary wooden house before his father's brick mansion was completed. His family moved into the brick mansion when Albert was five years old. Since Albert's brothers and his sister attended a school conducted on the estate by a tutor, Albert begged to attend school with them, even though he was very young. His nurse carried Albert along with Albert's beloved cat. (Cat's name unknown.) Supposedly the nurse carried Albert and the cat on a large, soft pillow.

Albert's mother, Jeannette Jenkins, died in 1843 when Albert was only 13 years old.

Albert Gallatin attended the Marshall Academy a few years after the two-story brick building was completed. It stood on the knoll where Marshall University now stands in Huntington. Albert paid $30.00 to board with a "respectable family" in the Guyandotte area. He was almost 15 years old when he reported for his first day of classes on Oct. 1, 1845. Albert's roommate at Marshall was Henderson Miller from Mason County. The two boys became close friends, and Albert was later best man at Henderson Miller's wedding. Their principal at the academy was the Rev. Josiah B. Poage. Poage was principal from 1843 to 1850, and was a Princeton graduate. Here, young Albert displayed the same energy and determination he had shown while studying before coming to the academy. He had a brilliant record in the sciences, mathematics, composition, elocution and languages. At that time, the Academy drew students from Kentucky, Ohio, and (western) Virginia. It is likely that Albert's brothers, William A. and Thomas Jefferson, attended Marshall Academy at this same time.

Contrary to earlier sources, Albert did not go on to attend Virginia Military Institute and receive military training.

Albert Jenkins grew up at the time when his father's plantation was in its most productive period. He no doubt learned to ride well, as his father and brothers had several head of horses and cattle on the estate. His family entertained many prominent citizens of the area at their fine home on the Ohio River.

EDUCATION: 1846-1850

After their schooling at Marshall Academy near Guyandotte, it was decided that the three Jenkins brothers would attend Jefferson College in Canonsburg, Pa. Jefferson was a men's college that had grown out of Canonsburg Academy, which was originally chartered in 1794. It was rechartered as Jefferson College in 1802. The normal undergraduate course of study in the 1840s was two years. The college is now known as Washington and Jefferson College, and is located in Washington, Pa.

In 1846 the three brothers boarded a steamboat that carried them to Jefferson College. They found room and board in Canonsburg at Brown's Boarding House. While there, Albert Gallatin excelled in his studies. He studied Latin Grammar, Roman Antiquities, Greek Grammar, Latin Composition, Horace, Livy, Tacitus, Demosthenes, Herodotus, National Philosophy, Meteorology, Geology, Algebra, Political Philosophy and English Composition. He was also one of the early members of the Phi Gamma Delta fraternity. Contrary to earlier sources, Albert was not one of the founders of the fraternity. There were six founding members of the fraternity at Jefferson in 1848, and Albert Gallatin Jenkins was the 11th member. Therefore, he was the 5th member after the founders.

While at Jefferson, Albert became interested in debating. These college debates gave him confidence in his public speaking ability. This would be a talent that would serve him well in his later life.

Albert graduated from Jefferson College on June 14, 1848. Because of his outstanding achievements, he was asked to deliver one of the commencement speeches. The exact content of that speech has been lost, but its title was "The Mystery of Nature." Probably his two brothers, Thomas Jefferson and William Alexander, were in the audience that heard Albert Gallatin's speech. Thomas Jefferson Jenkins and William Alexander Jenkins also graduated from Jefferson College in 1848.

After their graduation from Jefferson, the three brothers headed back to the Homestead at Greenbottom. While spending the summer of 1848 there, a fraternity brother of Albert's stopped at the Homestead to visit him. This friend was John Templeton McCarty. McCarty had been the leader of the six young men who founded Phi Gamma Delta at Jefferson College. McCarty said later in a letter to another founder that he: ". . . shook him (Jenkins) warmly by the hand and expressed many wishes for his future glory. . . ." Supposedly it was due to McCarty's encouragement that Albert decided to continue his studies by attending Harvard Law School at Cambridge, Mass.

Albert Gallatin Jenkins enrolled at Harvard on Sept. 28, 1848. He roomed for his first year at Mr. Torry's Boarding House. The course of study in law at Harvard at that time was also two years. His studies included Common Law, Commercial, International and Constitutional Law, as well as lectures on history. Moot or mock courts were held each week, with the students arguing cases. Albert Jenkins amassed a large library containing many books on the Greek and Roman classics, philosophers, and the law. He maintained this extensive library up until the time of his death.

In Albert's senior year at Harvard, his address was No. 15 Graduate's Hall. He graduated from Harvard with a LL.B. degree on July 17, 1850. That same year he was admitted to the bar.

When Albert returned to Greenbottom in the summer of 1850, he renewed his acquaintance with George W. Summers. Summers had become one of the outstanding lawyers of western Virginia. Jenkins and Summers later became law partners for a short period of time.

To broaden his perspective, Albert and his father agreed that a trip to South America would be in order. In the summer of 1850, Albert sailed to that area and visited several countries after his graduation from Harvard. He supposedly visited many of the same ports that his father had done business in through the years. An article published in London during the Civil War hinted that Albert had participated in helping some of the people of South America in their struggle against despotism while on this trip, but no further evidence can be found to support this.

LAW AND POLITICAL CAREER: 1850-1861

When Albert Gallatin Jenkins returned home from his trip to South America in the latter half of the year 1850, he decided to actively take up the practice of law. He began his practice of law at Charleston, later the capital city of West Virginia. We do not know whether he started out in practice by himself, or immediately sought to join in a partnership with a senior lawyer. During the next few years, however, Albert did join in partnership with George W. Summers, one of the outstanding legal figures of this part of Virginia. Summers was one of the most experienced and intelligent debators of the time, and Jenkins no doubt picked up a few pointers from the elder lawyer. This partnership continued at least until 1852, when Summers was elected judge of the Kanawha Circuit Court. Summers had been a U. S. Congressman in 1841, and had been an unsuccessful candidate from the Whig Party for governor in 1851. George W. Summers was later a delegate to the secession convention from Kanawha County, but voted against secession. During this period of time, Albert also maintained a small office that he and his father had built adjoining the Homestead at Greenbottom.

Albert did not devote all his time to his law profession during the early 1850s. He also assisted his aging father in managing the farm at Greenbottom. Albert's sister Eustatia had already married and left home. Even though Thomas Jefferson was still single, he was living in a small house on the estate separate from the Homestead. William Alexander married in 1853. We do know that Albert spent much time at the Homestead during this period and assisted in managing the estate.

Also during this time, Albert became interested in politics and public service. His father and brothers were strong Democrats and evidently spoke out many times at local gatherings. The Republican Party was a rising star with vigorous leaders and presented a strong challenge; therefore, the Democratic Party was also looking for new blood and young leadership. This was an ideal environment for a young, educated lawyer who enjoyed debating. Albert Jenkins began to make a few speeches in public, and to have political discussions with influential political friends of his family.

By the spring of 1856, the political situation was highly confused. There were three Democratic candidates for the presidential nomination: President Franklin Pierce, Stephen A. Douglas, and James Buchanan. This was also the first time that the Republican Party had a candidate. This was John C. Fremont. The Whig Party joined forces with the American and the Know-Nothing parties to nominate ex-President Millard Fillmore. By then Albert G. Jenkins was recognized as one of the brilliant spokesmen for the Democratic cause. Albert displayed much personal charm and a very logical method of delivery of his material. He also began making it known that he wanted to be a delegate to the Democratic National Convention.

Jenkins became very popular in the Cabell County area, and was well known by the time a mass meeting was held at Barboursville in March of 1856. At that time, Barboursville was the county seat of Cabell. The meeting was presided over by Lt. Gov. E. W. McComas, and the meeting ended with Albert G. Jenkins being nominted as a candidate for delegate to the Democratic National Convention. The next month, in April, a district convention of the Democratic Party met in Charleston. It formally named Albert Gallatin Jenkins as the delegate from this area to the national convention to be held in Cincinnati.

Later in 1856, Jenkins decided to run for a seat in Congress. Then came a long series of appearances and debates. One of the highlights of the campaign for that year occurred on Sept. 20, 1856. On that date Jenkins participated in a long debate held at Hurricane Bridge in Putnam County, with Congressman John S. Carlile. Jenkins made many strong points, gave the floor to Carlile for rebuttal, and then came back with a very strong closing. The Charleston, Va., "Kanawha Valley Star" reported: "The enthusiasm of the Democracy was perfectly unbounded, and toward the close of Mr. Jenkins' speech surpassed everything that we have witnessed. He is a young man of superior intellect and is likely to make a statesman of the first order."

John S. Carlile was later also a member of the secession convention. He left Richmond, however, and returned home where he began a "new-state" movement. This led to the 1st Wheeling Convention which also led eventually to the formation of the state of West Virginia.

Later that year, on Dec. 4, 1856, the Democratic Congressional convention met in Parkersburg to choose who would run against John S. Carlile. Isaac Ong was one of the delegates from Cabell County and traveled there with Albert Jenkins. Ong was a friend of Jenkins' and was later one of the original members of the Border Rangers militia company, detailed in later chapters. The race came down to Jenkins and William L. Jackson of Wood County. This Jackson was a cousin of the famous "Stonewall" and later became himself a general in the Confederate Army, and was nicknamed "Mudwall." Jackson finally withdrew as a candidate and, therefore, Jenkins was nominated by default. For some reason lost in time, Jenkins first rose before the group and declined, but after Mr. F. P. Turner moved that Jenkins be nominated by acclamation, Jenkins accepted the nomination.

The first part of 1857 was dedicated to campaigning, and election day soon arrived. It was to be held the 4th Thursday in May, and it fell on the 28th. Albert G. Jenkins opposed John S. Carlile for the seat in the 35th Congress. The election was held and the "Kanawha Valley Star" of June 2nd announced the results. Albert G. Jenkins received 550 votes from Cabell County against 335 for John Carlile. The largest vote was in Harrison County, which cast 853 votes for Jenkins and 726 for Carlile. But the final totals read: Jenkins–7,752 votes and Carlile–6,773 votes. Albert Gallatin Jenkins was the new Congressman from Cabell County!

Before Jenkins took his seat in Washington, a strange occurrence took place along the Ohio River. In the summer of 1857 Eli Thayer from Massachusetts, who had also been elected to the House of Representatives, made a visit to the Ceredo area. Ceredo was a few miles downriver from Guyandotte. Thayer believed that New England had

". . . an intelligent and active surplus population which must find an outlet." Thayer wanted to move workers, mechanics, and builders from New England to set up colonies all the way to Kansas. These small colonies were to be focal points for the battle against slavery. Ceredo was to be one of Thayer's colonies. He wished to colonize that area also due to the availability of cheap land. Thayer had organized a group known as the "Northern Emigrant Aid Society" to import the free white labor into Virginia. Many residents of the Ceredo area in northern Wayne County did support Thayer and his colony. They viewed this influx as a boon to the area's economy. Needless to say, Thayer's project was viewed by many Cabell Countians with distaste. As a result, angry residents of the area traveled to Greenbottom to see their new congressman, Albert G. Jenkins. In August of 1857, Jenkins went to Ceredo and confronted Thayer's followers and organizers. Thayer spoke out against Jenkins, calling him: ". . . a spectator-spy; a fire-eating slaveholder." A protest meeting was held at 4 p.m. on August 26 at the Town Hall in Guyandotte. Present were many supporters and friends of Jenkins, such as Isaac Ong, John Everett, Dr. Ricketts, and L. Sedinger. Here Jenkins spoke out against Thayer and his "Ceredo Plan." Thayer, of course, struck back by accusing Jenkins of gathering up some "bar-room loafers" and relatives and trying to "extinguish the colony." Jenkins also wrote a letter on August 13 to Gov. Henry A. Wise protesting the colony. Wise contended that the whole situation did not concern him at all. The local dispute between the two men ended when both Jenkins and Thayer went to Washington to be sworn in at the opening session of the 35th Congress on Dec. 7, 1857. Due to much local opposition, Thayer's colony idea eventually died, probably aided by the rumor that Thayer had unknowingly supplied guns to John Brown prior to Brown's raid on Harper's Ferry. A few of the northerners did remain at Ceredo, however. These emigrants remained supporters of the Union, and supplied many of the men recruited into the Union Army from the Ceredo area.

When Jenkins first arrived in Washington, he lived at Crutchet's Boarding House, located at the corner of D Street. As a freshman member of Congress, his seat was toward the rear of the large room in the south wing of the Capitol Building. Jenkins' seat was at desk number 172.

During adjournments of Congress, Jenkins went to St. Louis to visit his brother, Dr. William A. Jenkins. On one of these trips, he began dating Miss Virginia Southard Bowlin.

Jenkins served in Washington until Congress adjourned on June 14, 1858. He immediately took a trip west to St. Louis, where he married Virginia Southard Bowlin on July 15, 1858. Virginia's father, James Butler Bowlin, was one of the prominent citizens of Missouri. He had been a district attorney and a judge of the criminal court and later served four terms in the House of Representatives from 1843 to 1851. He had also been the United States' representative in Columbia and Paraguay. It has been suggested that Albert Jenkins' trip to South America in 1850 had some connection with James Bowlin's position on that continent. Perhaps this is how Albert and Virginia first met.

The "Kanawha Valley Star" of Aug. 3, 1858, reported the joyous occasion on the social page in this manner:

> We announce today the marriage of our friend Mr. Jenkins, the Representative of this district in Congress to Miss Bowlin of St. Louis. The happy and distinguished pair passed through this place on Thursday on their way to White Sulphur Springs, where they will spend the hot months of summer.

CLAYTON-BULWER TREATY.

SPEECH

OF

HON. ALBERT G. JENKINS

OF VIRGINIA,

ON FOREIGN RELATIONS,

Delivered in the House of Representatives, January 12, 1859.

The House being in Committee of the Whole on the state of the Union—

Mr. JENKINS said:

Mr. Chairman: I had hoped, after the recess which both Houses have taken during the holydays, and in consideration of the short intervening period from this date to the adjournment of Congress, that debate would be confined to subjects affecting the real interests of the Republic at home, and her reputation abroad. I confess, sir, that I have been disappointed in this respect by the speech of the gentleman from Maine, [Mr. WASHBURN,] who was last upon the floor. It was, for the most part, the same old thing of slavery and anti-slavery; Lecompton and anti-Lecompton. I can see no excuse for the constant harangues upon this topic to the utter neglect of the vital interests of the Confederacy, both domestic and foreign. But, sir, so it is. If the tariff is to be raised, these gentlemen of the Republican party think the only way to enlighten themselves and the country, preparatory to so doing, is by reading long essays against the institutions of their brethren of the South. If matters affecting our foreign interests are to be acted on, they seem to think the only legitimate manner of approaching the subject is through a speech denouncing the "slave oligarchy." Like Dr. Sangrado, who persisted in his specific of "bleeding and warm water" for all ailments, however different, so our political doctors of the Republican party dose us with anti-slavery speeches for all the ills that afflict the body politic. A remarkable point of similitude in the two cases is the pertinacity which each has displayed in adhering to their practice. Would it be hazarding too much, sir, to surmise that it was for the same reason in each case? The former, you recollect, not only made himself great and famous by it, but also found his bread and butter in it, "which," says his historian, "was of much more importance to him than the health of his patients" I think, sir, it would not be uncharitable to conclude that similar considerations have their weight with our anti-slavery agitators. I shall not consume the time which I have allotted myself for the discussion of other topics, by any further notice of the speech of the gentleman from Maine, [Mr. WASHBURN.] I merely want the country to know, in case we adjourn leaving any matters of necessary legislation unattended to, where the blame rests.

And now, sir, I revert with pleasure to the subject of our foreign relations, upon which my distinguished friend from Missouri [Mr. ANDERSON] was so felicitous in his remarks yesterday. That the foreign policy of a country like ours should constantly attract the attention of its citizens, is necessarily consequent upon the character of its free institutions.

Commencing with the origin of our Govern

Copy of first page of speech given by Albert G. Jenkins on foreign policy to the House of Representatives, Jan. 12, 1859.

Albert Jenkins and his bride returned to Washington for the remainder of the session of the 35th Congress. Congress convened in the first part of December 1858, and Jenkins was back in action. He gained the reputation as a dangerous man to tangle with in a debate on the floor. Albert Jenkins' first full-dress speech before Congress was delivered on Jan. 12, 1859. Jenkins chose foreign policy and the Clayton-Bulwer Treaty as his topic for this speech, which came as a welcome change from the endless oratory on the slavery question. He remarked that the endless debates on the slavery issue were useless. Jenkins here outlined his support of the Monroe Doctrine in Latin America. He proposed motions that America take more active steps to bar foreign nations from making inroads into the western hemisphere. Toward the end of his speech, he mentioned that the state of Virginia was planning to erect a statue to James Monroe in Richmond. He urged that honor be paid to Monroe ". . . not by developing in the marble its latent forms of beauty. . . . But let us do it by incorporating into our foreign policy, as a fundamental principle, the doctrine already consecrated by his name." He closed with the Latin phrase: "Exergi monumentum, oere perennium." Translated, this becomes: "I have built a monument more enduring than brass." This speech was well received, and "The Washington Statesman" commented on Jan. 14, 1859, that "We accept it as a good omen for the country that Congress is beginning to bestow attention on the external relations of the government." The editorial went on to state, "The speech of Mr. Jenkins especially is a most opportune vindication of American policy." The "Kanawha Valley Star" carried the speech in total on the front page of its issue of Feb. 1, 1859.

Albert G. Jenkins now had to turn his thoughts and energy back to the political campaign. His two-year term in Congress was drawing to a close, and he was determined to run for re-election. He was once again facing the "4th Thursday in May."

In March of 1859, at a convention held in Parkersburg, Jenkins was nominated as a candidate for re-election to the National Congress. Now the trail of speeches and debates began again. The high point of this campaign was a debate held in Weston on May 9, 1859. Over 800 people turned out to witness the debate between James M. Laidley and Jenkins. Laidley was an older and more experienced speaker than Jenkins. But seldom had the old courthouse heard a more masterful presentation than that of Jenkins. "The Weston Herald," on the following Monday, commented that Mr. Laidley was no match for the Hon. Albert G. Jenkins in a public discussion, and noted that the "Democracy is delighted with him." When the fateful Thursday in May came, Jenkins polled a vote of 668, to Laidley's 248. Jenkins had now won a seat in the 36th Congress!

Albert's success in the election was dimmed, however, with the realization that his father was growing weaker every day. As autumn came, Congressman Jenkins stayed close to Greenbottom to be near his father, who had been a strong supporter of his son's political career. Capt. William Jenkins died on Nov. 17, 1859, and was buried in a cast iron vault in the family plot at Greenbottom next to Albert's mother.

Albert and his two brothers were all named joint executors of William's will. Under this will, Albert inherited the Homestead, Thomas Jefferson inherited the middle third of the estate, and Dr. William A. inherited the lower portion of the Greenbottom estate. Their sister, Eustacia, received a large bequest in cash and Capt. William's house and lot in Lynchburg.

Finally, Albert and his wife, Virginia, returned to Washington for the first session of the 36th Congress. They were also expecting their first child, who arrived on Jan. 29, 1860. He was named James Bowlin Jenkins.

Albert G. Jenkins showed his political awareness in a letter dated Feb. 28, 1860. He spoke both of the upcoming Democratic presidential primary and of his new son:

Washington, D. C. Feb. 28th 1860.

My Dear sir,

I have for some days been promising myself the pleasure of replying to your kind letter of the 10th inst, but in the press & hurry of other matters seemed never to have a leisure moment in which to do so.

I agree with you with reference to the necessity of keeping our people posted & enlightened upon the issues which now so unhappily threaten the peace of the country. Living as they do upon the border of a border state and having scarcely enough of the institution of slavery in their midst to justify the name; it is apparent that it will be an inviting point of attack on the part of northern fanaticism which is always vigilant & keen-sighted in its attempts to undermine the social system of the south by poisoning & corrupting the sentiment of such of her people as can be thus influenced. And it is not to be concealed that their efforts in Western Virginia in this respect have not been entirely without success.

There is a proposition now pending in our body to reduce our mileage to about one fourth of its present amount. I think it will pass. Our present mileage you know is forty cents a mile going & coming.

I think it also highly probable that the franking privilege will be abolished during the present session.

There is of course at this time great efforts made towards the "manufactory" of presidents, at Washington—as this seems to be a sort of political centre, towards which all the political elements gravitate. Douglas will undoubtedly go into the Charleston Convention with the largest vote. I believe too that he will ultimately command a majority of all the votes in the convention, but I doubt his ability under any circumstances to concentrate upon himself *two thirds*.

But changing the subject somewhat, I must not forget to tell you before I close that I have a fine boy four weeks old. Of course we all think him the greatest fellow in the world.

I shall be glad to hear from you at all times & remain

Truly your friend,
A. G. Jenkins

To: Hon. G. D. Camden

Meanwhile, matters in the 36th Congress had become grim and tense. All of official Washington now realized that a real crisis was unavoidable. Albert Jenkins was deeply concerned about the future of the union. In another full-dress speech before the House on April 26, 1860, he stated:

There is no denying the fact, Mr. Chairman, that we are rapidly approaching a crisis in the history of the Republic; a crisis which must culminate for weal or woe in a few brief months; for within that time, it must be decided into whose hands the control of the Federal Government will pass for the next four years, and upon what principles it will be administered. We, of the South, believe that, should the Republican party be successful in obtaining control of this Government, including the Chief Executive office, such a state of things would seriously impair our rights and threaten the permanency of our institutions.

THE SLAVERY QUESTION.

SPEECH OF HON. A. G. JENKINS,

OF VIRGINIA,

IN THE HOUSE OF REPRESENTATIVES, APRIL 26, 1860.

The House being in the Committee of the Whole on the state of the Union—

Mr. JENKINS said:

Mr. CHAIRMAN: I have heretofore invariably confined my remarks to existing subjects of legislation legitimately before this body for legislative action. And even now, sir, I do not propose to avail myself of the latitude of debate allowed in the Committee of the Whole on the state of the Union, to discuss irrelevant matters, as is often done by members of this House; for, sir, the *state of the Union* is the very subject upon which I propose to speak, definitely and pertinently, if I can.

We have all seen the time, sir, when the state of the Union, so far at least as affected the question of its perpetuity, did not occasion a single perturbed thought to any one individual within the limits of the Republic. But now, sir, we know it to furnish a subject of serious and anxious contemplation for millions, whose apprehensions for its integrity and preservation I trust may not be too well founded.

There is no denying the fact, Mr. Chairman, that we are rapidly approaching a crisis in the history of the Republic; a crisis which must culminate for weal or woe in a few brief months; for within that time, it must be decided into whose hands the control of the Federal Government will pass for the next four years, and upon what principles it will be administered. We, of the South, believe that, should the Republican party be successful in obtaining control of this Government, including the Chief Executive office, such a state of things would seriously impair our rights and threaten the permanency of our institutions. On the other hand, the Republicans affect to believe that the prolonged ascendency of the Democratic party would inflict just such calamities upon the people, and their institutions, of the North.

It will then be in the most natural order of the subject to consider—

1. Would the triumph of the Republican party in the next presidential contest furnish the South with ground for serious apprehension and alarm?

2. Would the continued ascendency of the Democratic party furnish the North with just ground for similar apprehension?

In considering the former of these propositions, we must first notice the fact that the North is in a majority in this Government. Having a majority of States, there is necessarily a majority of northern Senators in the other wing of the Capitol; and having a majority of representative population, there is a consequent northern majority of Representatives upon this floor. And when, as in the case supposed, you shall elect a Republican President, it will almost inevitably follow that the same manifestation of popular sentiment will convert the present northern majority in this body into a purely Republican majority; and it is but fair to presume that it will finally accomplish the same result in the Senate. Indeed, this is the avowed object of the Republican party. Then, sir, with a Republican President, a Republican Senate, and a Republican House, we will witness the admintration of the Government upon the principles of the Republican party. And what are they? Without stopping at this time to enunciate them in the full and exact phraseology of the various editions of its platforms, and without meaning to be so illiberal as to make the extreme views of some of the Republican party the common standard of measurement for all the members of your organization, yet your whole creed, and *all* your principles may be comprised in a nut-shell—*antagonism to the institution of negro slavery.*

This is the Alpha and Omega—the beginning and the end. Upon this principle of hostility to the institutions of one section of the Confederacy, the other section proposes to administer the Government. Sir, this proposition of itself is so startling, so alarming, that

Polkinhorn, printer, 375 D st.

First page of speech delivered by Albert G. Jenkins before the House of Representatives on April 26, 1860, on "The Slavery Question."

Some other matters did come up before this Congress, other than the gathering storm of slavery and states' rights. One issue was the tariff bill of 1860. Congressman Jenkins delivered another striking speech on May 8, 1860, in which he stated: "By reducing the duties upon luxuries, and increasing them upon necessaries, you throw the whole burden of supporting the Government upon the laboring men. I propose to increase the duties upon luxuries, and diminish them upon articles of necessity."

The year 1860 finally drew to a close. Now tensions in Congress between the Northern and Southern factions rose in intensity with the approaching inauguration of President Abraham Lincoln. On Jan. 18, 1861, Jenkins introduced an amendment to the Army Appropriation Bill, which specified that no money could be used to recapture any forts, arsenals or navy yards from states seceding from the Union. By this time South Carolina had become the first state to secede from the Union, and it was obvious that others would follow.

The 36th Congress drew to a close. Congressman Albert G. Jenkins cast his last recorded vote on March 1, 1861. The motion was to allow a Mr. Williamson to collect $1,000 for his time and mileage spent in an unsuccessful contest to unseat Congressman Dan Sickles of New York. Congress officially came to an end on either March 3 or March 4, 1861. By that time, seven southern states had seceded from the Union. Virginia, however, was still holding out through the congressional election to be held in the spring.

The Democratic nominating convention for congressional candidates met in Parkersburg on March 28. Twelve days before, on March 16, Jenkins had penned a regretful letter from Greenbottom to the convention. In it he stated that he had received

The U. S. House of Representatives chamber in Washington, circa 1861. Albert G. Jenkins' seat is shown in the circle.

numerous letters and had had several conversations with many persons in which he had expressed his desire not to be a candidate for re-election to Congress. He finished with: ". . . I shall carry with me an undying devotion to those principles of States Rights Democracy, whose success I have ever believed to be necessary to preserve the rights and liberties of the people." This letter was ignored by some delegates who made the motion that Jenkins again be nominated by acclamation. This was immediately carried out even in his absence.

Even as late as April 9, 1861, the "Kanawha Valley Star" was still publishing on its front page: "For Congress, Hon. Albert G. Jenkins, of Cabell." A long editorial in that issue put high distinctions on Jenkins and spoke of his high morality and stated:

> A very general appreciation of these services, and this disposition for loyalty, has marked him out, almost without competition, and against his own wishes, as deserving of reappointment to the leadership. . . .

A world-shaking event occurred, however, to settle the issue of Jenkins' candidacy. On April 12, 1861, the war officially started with the bombardment of Fort Sumter. A few days later Virginia seceded from the Union. Now there would be no representatives sent from Virginia to the Congress of the United States.

Albert Jenkins' dream of further serving his state and country as a lawyer and congressman would never be realized. As war loomed on the horizon, his leadership would now turn to one of the military instead of political.

Albert G. Jenkins while he was brigadier general of Confederate cavalry. Circa 1862-64.
Courtesy: National Archives

MILITARY CAREER: 1861

With the fate of Virginia now decided, Albert G. Jenkins remained at home at Greenbottom. While the clouds of war hung over the land, Albert Jenkins was once again happily blessed. On April 5, 1861, Albert and Virginia's second child was born. She was named Alberta Gallatin after her famous father. His happy days at home were numbered, however. On April 20, 1861, there was a gathering of the local militia units and the people of Guyandotte in front of the Planter's Hotel. The largest and probably the only organized militia unit present was the Border Rangers. This unit had been formed on Dec. 10, 1860, to protect a Virginia flag raised in front of the Planter's Hotel. We have found no records of any other activities of the Border Rangers between its date of formation in 1860 and April 20, 1861. On April 20, another flag ". . . made by the secession ladies of Guyandotte" was hoisted up the flagpole. A young country boy who was there that day related the incidents as follows. While walking to town to get his mail, he met a young lady wearing an apron that was very ununsual to him. The pattern on her apron was supposedly exactly the same as the strange flag flying from the flagpole. The boy said, "We were struck with the new emblems, but were slow to take in the significance of the same." Just then a large side-wheeled steamboat, the "Ohio No. 3," came down the river and docked at the Guyandotte landing. This boat brought the fateful news that the Virginia Convention had passed the ordinance of secession. Deafening shouts arose for a few moments and then silence. Soon the boat pulled out from the dock and was gone. The young boys took a seat on the sidewalk in front of the hotel on the side next to the river. While still considering the mystery of the new flag, they heard something strike the brick wall of the hotel just over their heads. They determined that it was from a gun fired from the opposite shore of the Ohio River. They immediately moved around the corner of the hotel. They ". . . became satisfied that the flag meant more than a sentiment, and the bullet more than a man's joke. . . ."

Before the crowd had dispersed, Albert G. Jenkins had ridden to town and addressed the militia groups. The Border Rangers then followed him to Greenbottom with what arms they could gather, mainly shotguns. There they ate their dinners and went into camp.

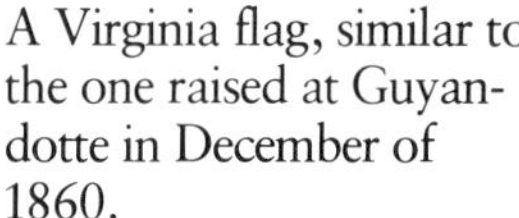
A Virginia flag, similar to the one raised at Guyandotte in December of 1860.

While camped there, the "Ironton Register" newspaper of Ironton, Ohio (definitely of Union sentiment), published the following article:

> We learn also that Hon. A. G. Jenkins, late member of Congress, is forming a Secession camp at his place, Green Bottom, above Guyandotte—providing quarters for a band of Secession soldiers, already having the corn and meat with which to feed them. He is now in Eastern Virginia, to procure arms.

After camping at Greenbottom a few weeks, the Border Rangers moved their camp to the old Green Bottom Baptist Church. Here they were joined by a group of recruits from Mason County, just north of Greenbottom. Here the men drilled and stayed in camp.

After about three weeks in camp at the Greenbottom Church, the Border Rangers were ordered to march to the Kanawha Valley. They stopped along the way at a farm owned by a Mr. Hall at Buffalo in Putnam County. Mr. Hall provided food for both the men and their horses. There was a small recruitment camp at Buffalo commanded by John McCausland, a pre-war graduate of the Buffalo Academy. We are not sure whether all the men in the unit had horses at this time or if a few were on foot. The next morning the men started for Coalsmouth, now known as St. Albans. Here about the first of May, Col. Christopher Q. Tompkins had set up a recruitment camp for the Confederate volunteers of that area. The camp was located just west of the mouth of Coal River. Here the men went into camp and according to Pvt. James D. Sedinger: ". . . drilled cavalry drill and thought we could whip the world." It was here on May 20, 1861, that the company was organized and officers were elected. Albert G. Jenkins was elected captain to replace Ira J. McGinnis, the original captain of the militia company in 1860. James D. Sedinger, who was elected third corporal, kept a diary throughout the entire war, and reported on that date 101 men reported for roll call.

While at Camp Tompkins, as the camp at Coalsmouth was named, the Border Rangers enjoyed various home-cooked foods. Sedinger noted in his diary:

> Our commissary department was looked after by the ladies of Cabell and Mason counties who kept us well supplied with boiled ham and roasted chicken, baked light bread and biscuit, cake and pies. Everything that they could think of to tickle the palate and we enjoyed ourselves better than we ever did afterwards.

As other volunteer units began to filter in to Camp Tompkins, the cavalry units grew to four. Now present were: the Border Rangers from Cabell County, the Sandy Rangers from Wayne County, the Fayette Rangers from Fayette County, and the Kanawha Rangers from Kanawha County. These units were all placed under the command of Capt. Jenkins. The Fayette Rangers were later placed back under Col. Tompkins and became Co. C of the 22nd Virginia Infantry on its formation. Up to this time, all these volunteer units were part of the Virginia State forces. On May 29, all these units were sworn into service in the Confederate Army.

During this time, Captain Jenkins studied military tactics. Since he had no previous military training, he learned along with his green recruits. He studied the basic training manual for both sides in the conflict. This was *Rifle and Light Infantry Tactics* by William J. Hardee. This volume showed marching formations and drilling exercises.

During their stay at Camp Tompkins, the cavalry, under their young captain,

HARDEE'S

RIFLE AND LIGHT INFANTRY

TACTICS,

FOR THE INSTRUCTION, EXERCISES AND MANŒUVRES OF

RIFLEMEN AND LIGHT INFANTRY.

INCLUDING

SCHOOL OF THE SOLDIER AND SCHOOL OF THE COMPANY.

BY BREVET LIEUT. W. J. HARDEE.

To which is added,
DUTIES OF NON-COMMISSIONED OFFICERS.

MILITARY HONORS TO BE PAID BY TROOPS.

THE ARTICLES OF WAR,

Containing Rules by which the Armies of the United States are governed;
Relating to Courts-Martial; Suppressing Mutiny or Sedition;
Granting Furloughs, Commissary of Musters; Accepting a
Challenge; Chaplains; Sutlers; To whom any Officer
may apply for Redress; Sentinels; False
Alarms; Misbehaviour; Making Known
the Watchword; Engineers; Spies;
How Courts-Martial must be
Authenticated, Etc.,

NEW YORK.

J. O. KANE, PUBLISHER, 126 NASSAU STREET.

1862.

Above: The sole source of military training for Albert G. Jenkins, when he entered Confederate service; Hardee's Rifle and Light Infantry Tactics was used by both sides as their basic training manual.

Above: A sequence from Hardee's chapter "School of the Soldier" (Left to right: "Load," "Prime," "Aim," and "Fire.")

The sole source of military training for Albert G. Jenkins, when he entered Confederate service. Hardee's *Rifle and Light Infantry Tactics* was used by both sides as their basic training manual. Author's collection began to provide some services that became the standard tasks of the cavalry during the war. They were dispatched from the camp to act as scouts.

While at Camp Tompkins, the Confederate units turned out on "dress parade" each evening. Many of the ladies of the area around Coalsmouth would turn out to watch these parades. Victoria Hansford Teays, who lived across from the camp, mentioned in her diary that they enjoyed listening to the brass band of the Kanawha Riflemen. As she went on to note,

> And now came those pleasant days. They seem like an oasis in a desert. . . . We seemed to forget the purpose for which they were here, or thought the evil hour far distant.

Soon after Albert Jenkins and his unit arrived at Coalsmouth, the ladies of that area made and presented his company with a flag. Victoria Hansford Teays' father, John Hansford, held the flag unfurled to the breeze while Miss Allie Lasley delivered a short speech to the company. Jenkins and his men were all mounted on their horses and pulled up along a fence under the shade of two large locust trees in the yard of the old hotel near the Coal River bridge. The ladies then showered the officers and men with bouquets of flowers. Captain Jenkins made a short acceptance speech and introduced Lucian "Cooney" Ricketts as "the child of the regiment." Ricketts was only 14 years old, and had followed the Confederates from Guyandotte. Captain Jenkins had tried in vain to talk Ricketts into returning home. After his persistence, Jenkins and the cavalry adopted him by unanimous vote. Ricketts brought his little mule with him, which had no saddle, and he supposedly rode at the head of the column, next to Jenkins.

Another incident which shows Jenkins' trust in Cooney Ricketts occured in May or June of 1861. Jenkins, finding that his cavalry units were sadly lacking in pistols, devised a plan to obtain a supply from Cincinnatti. Since pistols were not allowed to be sent from there to this or any other place in the South, someone would have to go to the source. Jenkins selected young Ricketts for the trip. He furnished Ricketts with money from his own pockets, and sent the boy on his way. Ricketts mounted his little mule and rode down to Guyandotte, where he boarded a steamer for Cincinnati. Once there, he purchased the needed weapons from several locations to avoid suspicion. He then scouted a Union camp near there, and returned to Coalsmouth with both weapons and intelligence information.

During the summer of 1861, Colonel Tompkins had formed three regiments from the 12 Confederate units at Camp Tompkins. These were known as the 1st, 2nd and 3rd Kanawha Regiments. Jenkins and his Border Rangers, along with the Fairview Rifle Guards from Wayne County, were attached to the 2nd Kanawha.

The first recorded expedition by Jenkins from Coalsmouth took place in June. Captain Jenkins and the Border Rangers rode north to Point Pleasant on the Ohio River. His group did not encounter any Union troops, but did take a number of Union sympathizers as prisoners. In retaliation the 21st Ohio Regiment, under Col. Jesse Norton, captured 30 secessionists to insure fair treatment of the men taken by Jenkins. Norton continued on to Greenbottom, where he raided the Jenkins farm and took corn and horses back with him to Gallipolis.

In July, a Union army unit under Lt. Col. George W. Neff encamped on the Jenkins farm at Greenbottom. While there, Colonel Neff told Mrs. Jenkins that if he (Neff) ever caught up with her husband, he would hang him from the nearest tree. Mrs.

The Cabell County courthouse on Main Street in Barboursville as it appeared during the War. It was erected about 1852. The building is now part of Barboursville Junior High School. The Cabell County seat was later moved to Huntington.
George S. Wallace Collection, courtesy Jane Wallace

Thornburg's Store on Main Street in Barboursville, as it appeared during the two skirmishes. Albert G. Jenkins supposedly stopped outside this store before the skirmish on July 14, 1861. George S. Wallace Collection, courtesy Jane Wallace

The 34th Ohio Volunteer Infantry marching down Main Street in Barboursville, Nov. 1861. Fortification Hill, site of the first skirmish of Barboursville, is just out of sight behind the courthouse in the upper right corner. George S. Wallace Collection, courtesy Jane Wallace

Jenkins supposedly said that if the two soldiers did meet, that her husband would certainly treat Neff as a gentleman.

On July 14, Colonel Neff and five companies of the 2nd Kentucky Regiment marched to the Cabell County seat of Barboursville. Here awaiting their arrival was a force of about 600 Confederates, including Jenkins' Border Rangers and the Sandy Rangers from Wayne County. Where Albert G. Jenkins was on that day is a mystery, as the Border Rangers was apparently commanded by Capt. Milton J. Ferguson. Mr. George E. Thornburg, who owned the store on main street in Barboursville, stated early in this century that he saw Captain Jenkins on the street opposite his store on that day. Thornburg related that an officer came up, and asked Jenkins if they were going to fight soldiers of the opposing side there. Jenkins supposedly stated: "Yes, but we must meet them outside of town. These folks here are our friends." The skirmish did take place just outside of town, at a knoll known as "Fortification Hill." After an exchange of gunfire between the two forces around the bridge over Mud River, the Confederates retreated back over the knoll through town. James Reynolds was the only Confederate killed. Three or four others were wounded. The Border Rangers and the Sandy Rangers evidently marched back to Camp Tompkins.

On July 16, scouts reported that the 2nd Kentucky was on the march toward the mouth of Scary Creek in Kanawha County. Some Virginia Confederate units were already in position near Scary Creek. On the morning of the 17th, Jenkins and the Border Rangers, along with Capt. Lewis' Kanawha Rangers, left Camp Tompkins and marched toward Scary. Captain Jenkins and his men proudly flew the flag presented to them by the ladies of Coalsmouth. This was the only flag at the Battle of Scary Creek, and it was shot to shreds by the end of the day's fighting.

The Confederate force at Scary now consisted of the 22nd Virginia Infantry under Lt. Col. George S. Patton, which also included Hale's Battery of artillery, company D of the 46th Virginia Infantry and the Border Rangers under Captain Jenkins.

The Union force consisted of the 12th and 21st Ohio Volunteer Infantry, Captain Cotter's Ohio Artillery, and Capt. John George's Independent Cavalry Co.

After an artillery barrage from both sides, a Union attack turned the right flank of the Confederate defenses. By 3 p.m. the Virginians began to retreat. At this point, Levi Welch of Hale's battery related:

> Captain Albert G. Jenkins, afterwards Brigadier General, came up the line of skirmishers, with his hat off and the blood streaming down his hair and neck, and called for someone to go and get his horse, tied to a stake behind Hale's Battery.

Young Welch, with some difficulty, did fetch Jenkins' horse. Jenkins mounted the horse and quickly rallied the Confederates. At about this time, Capt. Corns and his Sandy Rangers rode down the hill singing "Bullets and Steel." These two attacks were enough to turn the left flank of the Union line. The retreating Union force left Lt. Col. Neff wounded on the battlefield. Jenkins, however, assuming that the Federals had pulled back in order to mount another attack, also ordered a retreat from the field. For a few minutes, this left the battlefield deserted by both armies. Col. Frank Anderson, of the Confederate Wise Legion, who had his two companies on the extreme left flank, noted this and brought the retreating Confederates back to their defenses. This resulted in a Confederate victory at Scary Creek.

At dusk, Jenkins and a few other officers were mounted on a small knoll observing the battlefield. In the smoke and poor visibility, Col. Charles DeVilliers of the 11th Ohio and Colonel Woodruff, Capt. George Austin and Capt. John Hurd, all of the 2nd Kentucky, rode up to the Confederates, and thinking they were friends, said to Jenkins: "Well, you have given the Rebels a good sound thrashing today." The response was for the "damned Yankees" to surrender or they would have the "hell blown out of them." All the Union officers were sent to Libby Prison in Richmond. From there, Captain Hurd wrote home that he had been treated kindly by Captain Jenkins and General Wise, and "... the utmost courtesy, civility and every attention to our wants was carefully attended to. . . ."

The next day, Colonel Neff was found wounded on the battlefield, and Captain Jenkins was summoned. Jenkins took Neff by the hand, assured him he would be treated gentlemanly and ordered his wounds dressed. Colonel Neff was paroled about ten days after his rash statement to Mrs. Jenkins.

Captain Jenkins and the Border Rangers only stayed in the area of Scary and Coalsmouth for another three or four days. They then marched back to the area of Greenbottom, where Jenkins visited his family.

No. 40.

Special Requisition.

1861

July 30th For Capt. Je[illegible] Company "Border Rangers"
" Six [illegible] Knives
" Fifteen [illegible] Pans.

I certify that the above requisition is correct, and that the [illegible]cified are absolutely requisite for the public service, rendered so by the folg circumstances:

A. G. Jenkins

[illegible] the articles specified in the above requisition

Commanding.

Earliest known military document from the Civil War bearing the signature of Albert G. Jenkins. It is dated July 30, 1861, and was signed for "Capt. Jenkins Company Border Rangers." The requisition for camp knives and mess pans was probably written while in camp at White Sulphur Springs in Greenbrier County. Courtesy: National Archives

About July 19, Jenkins and his men sighted the steamer "Fannie McBrownie" (or McBurnie) steaming up the Ohio River. At this point the cavalry concealed their horses and hid themselves in a large paw paw thicket. Jenkins, without his uniform coat and with a carpet satchel in his hand, hailed the boat. The captain of the boat, assuming Jenkins to be a passenger, pulled into the bank. Jenkins then called loudly three times "Border Rangers!" As his men came yelling out of the thicket, the boat attempted to back out into the river. Jenkins drew his pistol and pointed it at the pilot's head and ordered him to hold the boat. The company took from the boat a case of swords and a few revolvers. The boat was then released and went on its way upriver.

The captain and his men camped a few more days near the captain's home. When the men mounted their horses to head back to Camp Tompkins, the Jenkins family accompanied them. The family rode in a carriage, followed by a wagon which contained their baggage.

When they arrived near Camp Tompkins, Jenkins was informed that Gen. Henry A. Wise had ordered a Confederate retreat from the Kanawha Valley. The Confederates then headed toward Lewisburg in Greenbrier County. The party, including the Jenkins family, evidently stayed for a short time on Paint Creek, between Charleston and Gauley Bridge. Victoria Hansford Teays recorded in her diary that the Jenkins family dined at her uncle Felix Hansford's house during this time. The Southerners arrived near Lewisburg and went into camp before the end of July.

During the month of August, 1861, the 8th Virginia Cavalry was organized from the Border Rangers, the Sandy Rangers, Lewis' Kanawha Rangers, and a few other cavalry companies. This occurred after Aug, 7, as on that date Jenkins signed a requisition for camp supplies as "Capt. Border Rangers." The exact date of organization is not known, but on that date in August, Capt. Corns was elected captain of one company, and Joseph Ferguson captain of another. Albert G. Jenkins resigned as captain and was elected colonel of the 8th Cavalry. The Border Rangers became Company E, Lewis's

BRIG. GEN. A. G. JENKINS.

Front page of the "Southern Illustrated News" of Oct. 3, 1863, featuring Brig. Gen. A.G. Jenkins.
Courtesy: Morrow Library, Marshall Univ.

Albert Gallatin Jenkins, probably while colonel of the 8th Virginia Cavalry, 1861-62.
From a drawing in the Library of Congress.

company (the Kanawha Rangers) became Company I, and Corns' Sandy Rangers became Company K. Jenkins' commission as lieutenant colonel dated officially from Sept. 24, 1861, as it had to be approved by the War Department in Richmond.

During the last weeks of August, Jenkins and his new regiment rode out on scouting missions from their camp near Lewisburg. On August 25th, Jenkins accidentally led his men into an ambush set up by the 11th Ohio Infantry at Piggott's Mill near Hawk's Nest. (This area is now a West Virginia State Park.) According to one account, Jenkins recklessly moved his men out ahead of the forward scouts, therefore exposing them. Jenkins' horse was shot and fell beneath him. One of his men was killed and three wounded. Jenkins himself narrowly avoided capture.

During this period the "Ironton Register" published another article, from information supplied by some of the Union troops that had passed through the Kanawha Valley:

> Jenkins (by parenthesis) is a genius. The Richmond papers teem with accounts of his prowess and personal daring, while to us he is an illusion, hovering just by our reach, aggravating us by his constant contiguity. . . . His company is unceasingly vigilant. . . .

Perhaps their experience near Piggott's Mill helped to increase this vigilance.

A few days later, the regiment was ordered out again on scout. This time they were to scout the area of Peters Creek in Nicholas County. Here they had a skirmish with the 7th Ohio Infantry. The regiment then camped near Kessler's Cross Lanes, where they took part in the battle there on August 26. They supported the 50th, 45th and 22nd Virginia Regiments.

For the next few days, the 8th Cavalry staged delaying actions against the advancing Union force under General Rosecrans. The men slowly fell back, and rode into the breastworks the Confederates had erected at Camp Gauley, near Carnifex Ferry. (Now a West Virginia Battlefield Park.) They arrived there on the 8th of September. Already there were two cavalry companies of the 50th Virginia, which would later become part of the 8th Virginia—the Smyth Dragoons and the Nelson Rangers. They later became companies A and B respectively of the 8th Cavalry. The Union force attacked the breastworks on September 10. After several frontal attacks, the Union force retired for the night. The Confederates, although suffering only seven men wounded, decided that the Union forces would be able to take the breastworks the next morning. Therefore, during the night, the Confederates moved their artillery down a narrow mountain trail, and the entire force moved across a pontoon bridge hastily erected at Carnifex Ferry. It has been debated if Colonel Jenkins was actually present at either the skirmish at Cross Lanes or the Battle of Carnifex Ferry. It is possible that he remained in the Lewisburg area to recruit. If so, then Corns or Colonel Jenifer was in command of the 8th Cavalry at Carnifex. A report of Sept. 30, 1861, did show the 8th Cavalry, attached to the Army of the Kanawha, as being commanded by Col. Walter H. Jenifer.

The 8th Cavalry then moved to Fayette Court House (now Fayetteville, W.Va.). They skirmished with Union forces along the area of Loup Creek over the next ten days.

Not much activity of Jenkins and his men is reported for the month of October. The weather in the Kanawha Valley was terrible. Heavy rains had fallen, and a bad winter was coming on. From some dispatches sending companies out as scouts, we know that Jenkins and the 8th Cavalry camped near Meadow Bluff in Greenbrier County during the month of October.

In early November, Gen. John B. Floyd determined to stage a raid in force through the western Virginia counties to the Ohio River. Guyandotte was selected as the target. In October, Col. K.V. Whaley (USA) had set up a recruitment camp there, and had about 150 recruits assembled. They were to form the 9th (West) Virginia Infantry, USA. Col. John Clarkson, commanding the Wise Legion Cavalry, and Colonel Jenkins, with the 8th Virginia Cavalry, formed the raiding party estimated at between 800 and 1,200 men. (The Ironton, Ohio "Register" gave the estimate as 800; later estimates suggest that closer to 1,200 is more accurate.) The Confederate cavalry left camp in Greenbrier County on Nov. 5. They marched by way of Chapmanville in Logan County and arrived at Guyandotte on Nov. 10. Due to a laxness on the part of the Union soldiers at the recruitment camp (known as Camp Paxton), no pickets were out and the camp was hit in total surprise. The Ironton "Register" commented that the townspeople had given Jenkins intelligence of the placement of troops, where their horses were stabled, etc. True or not, the surprise was still complete. The column reached the wire suspension bridge, and Jenkins and the Virginia Cavalry were among the first Confederates across. Sedinger recorded it thus in his diary:

> The Yanks were forming in companies on each side of the bridge against the railing. We went through them and dismounted on the west side of the bridge and formed at the end of the pier. About 5 minutes after forming the enemy concluded to cross and cut out. We waited until they were in 50 feet of us when we opened fire on them.

The suspension bridge at Guyandotte, Cabell County, as it appeared during the war. Jenkins and the Border Rangers clashed with the federal force on the left end of the bridge on Nov. 10, 1861. George S. Wallace Collection, courtesy Jane Wallace

Dashing in at a gallop, the attackers gave Whaley little time to rally his untrained recruits. Other pockets of Union troops fought from buildings and alleys. The overwhelming Confederate force soon overpowered the pockets of resistence and spent the rest of the night locating the Union recruits and troopers who were hiding in the town. Reports again vary, but the total captured appears to be about 100. The Ironton "Register" reported five Union soldiers killed and 10 wounded. Two Confederates were killed, one of them Capt. Tom Huddleston of the Kanawha Rangers.

At about 8 a.m. the next morning, the Jenkins-Clarkson force was alerted by the arrival of the steamer "Boston" bringing reinforcements to the Federals. Another 200 men of the 5th (West) Virginia Infantry were also approaching overland from Ceredo. The Confederates, however, had rounded up their prisoners and were just leaving town heading south. As the Union reinforcements arrived, they set fire to the town, claiming it was full of Rebel sympathizers. Along with the town, the Buffington Mill also burned. Thomas Jefferson Jenkins, Albert's brother, was part owner in this mill.

The rebel force, with about 100 prisoners marched south through Logan County. They stopped for a short rest at Wyoming Court House (now Pineville). For 12 days the march continued, over Flat Top Mountain and on to the railhead at Newbern, Va. There the prisoners were loaded on cattlecars for the remainder of their trip to Richmond. Eventually the military prisoners were exchanged and the civilians released.

Even though total casualities were very low, this incident was known in the north as "the massacre at Guyandotte."

From Newbern the regiment marched to Tazewell Court House, where they received orders to go into winter quarters at the Old Camp Meeting ground in Russell County.

MILITARY CAREER: 1862

The year of 1862 began with the majority of the 8th Cavalry being ordered into eastern Kentucky. Colonel Jenkins, with about 400 cavalrymen, moved west of Paintsville where they skirmished with some Union troops under the command of Col. James A. Garfield (later a U.S. president.)

In late January, the Border Rangers was back in Virginia, near Raleigh Court House (now Beckley.) Here, according to Sedinger, they were attacked by a Union force near the mouth of Bluestone River in present Summers County, W.Va. After a short skirmish, the Union force retired, much to the delight of the Confederates. It is not known whether or not Jenkins was present at this skirmish in Raleigh County.

While thus serving as regimental commander in the Confederate Army, Jenkins was elected to represent the 14th Virginia Congressional District in the first Confederate Congress. He therefore resigned as lieutenant colonel of the 8th Cavalry on Feb. 20, 1862. After his narrow escapes in 1861, this must have come as a relief to his wife and children. They now rode to Richmond and established themselves there. While serving in the Confederate Congress, Albert Jenkins was elected to the standing committees of Printing, and Territories and Public Lands.

On March 17, Jenkins leased to his father-in-law, James B. Bowlin, the Greenbottom estate. The lease was to run ten years. Bowlin was to perform services at the farm, and the farm was not to have more than 30 acres cultivated in any one season in grain, hemp or tobacco. It is not known if Bowlin actually occupied the farm at that time or later.

Richmond at that time was bustling with activity. It was not only the seat of the Confederate government but was also an important military headquarters. It was also one of the centers of social life in the South, even more so than before the war. Mr. and Mrs. Jenkins were again part of the important social and political circles, as they had been a part of the same scene in Washington only a year before.

During the month of July, 1862, influential men of the western Virginia counties submitted letters to the Confederate government in support of the promotion of Jenkins to the rank of brigadier general. Among those were Henry Fitzhugh, Allen T. Caperton, and Augustus A. Chapman. Henry Fitzhugh had been lieutenant colonel of the 8th Virginia Cavalry after Jenkins was elected to the Confederate Congress. Allen T. Caperton was a lawyer from Monroe County and a Yale graduate. He had been a state senator, a member of the constitutional convention, and a delegate to the secession convention. He was one of the most influential men in the Monroe and Mercer County area. Augustus Alexandria Chapman was also a lawyer and was also a member of the Virginia Assembly. At the start of the war, Chapman was a general of the Virginia Militia, having under his command the regiments from Giles, Monroe, and Greenbrier Counties. Chapman's letter was forwarded to Gen. Lee for his comments. Lee's comment on the back of this letter was: "During my service in the Kanawha Valley I considered Col. Jenkins (then Lt. Col. of Floyd's Cav) the best of the cav. officers."

By Aug. 5, Jenkins received his appointment as brigadier general of cavalry, and was ordered to report to Maj. Gen. W. W. Loring, then in Monroe County. Jenkins was to take command of the 8th and 14th Virginia Cavalry Regiments. Jenkins resigned his seat in the Confederate Congress on the same day. His appointment was confirmed in Richmond on Sept. 30, 1862. Jenkins joined his new brigade while it was encamped at Salt Sulphur Springs, Monroe County.

Gen. Loring saw an opportunity to strike against the Federals in the Kanawha and Ohio Valleys. He ordered Jenkins to compose a fast-moving strike force of cavalry. This unit would consist of seven companies of his old regiment, the 8th Virginia, and five companies under Capt. W. R. Preston. (These five companies under Preston had been organized into the 14th Virginia Cavalry.) The force, totaling about 550 men under Jenkins, left Salt Sulphur Springs on Aug. 20. The horsemen first headed north up the Tygart Valley. Their first encounter with the enemy was near Huttonsville, in Randolph County. Here the Jenkins command captured six Union scouts in order to determine the strength of the Federal outpost at Beverly. After questioning the prisoners, Jenkins decided instead to attack Buckhannon in Upshur County. There were several thousand small arms located there. To accomplish this, Jenkins split his command. He took the majority of the troops along a bridle path over Rich Mountain, while leaving the Border Rangers in the Tygart Valley to act as rear guard. Near Buckhannon, the force was fired upon by some "home guards," which were soon captured and dispersed.

Upon reaching Buckhannon Jenkins sent four companies through the woods around the town, while Colonel Corns and the other companies went down the main road to town. Preston and two companies remained in reserve. The Confederates routed the Federals and occupied the town on Aug. 30. Jenkins found the stand of

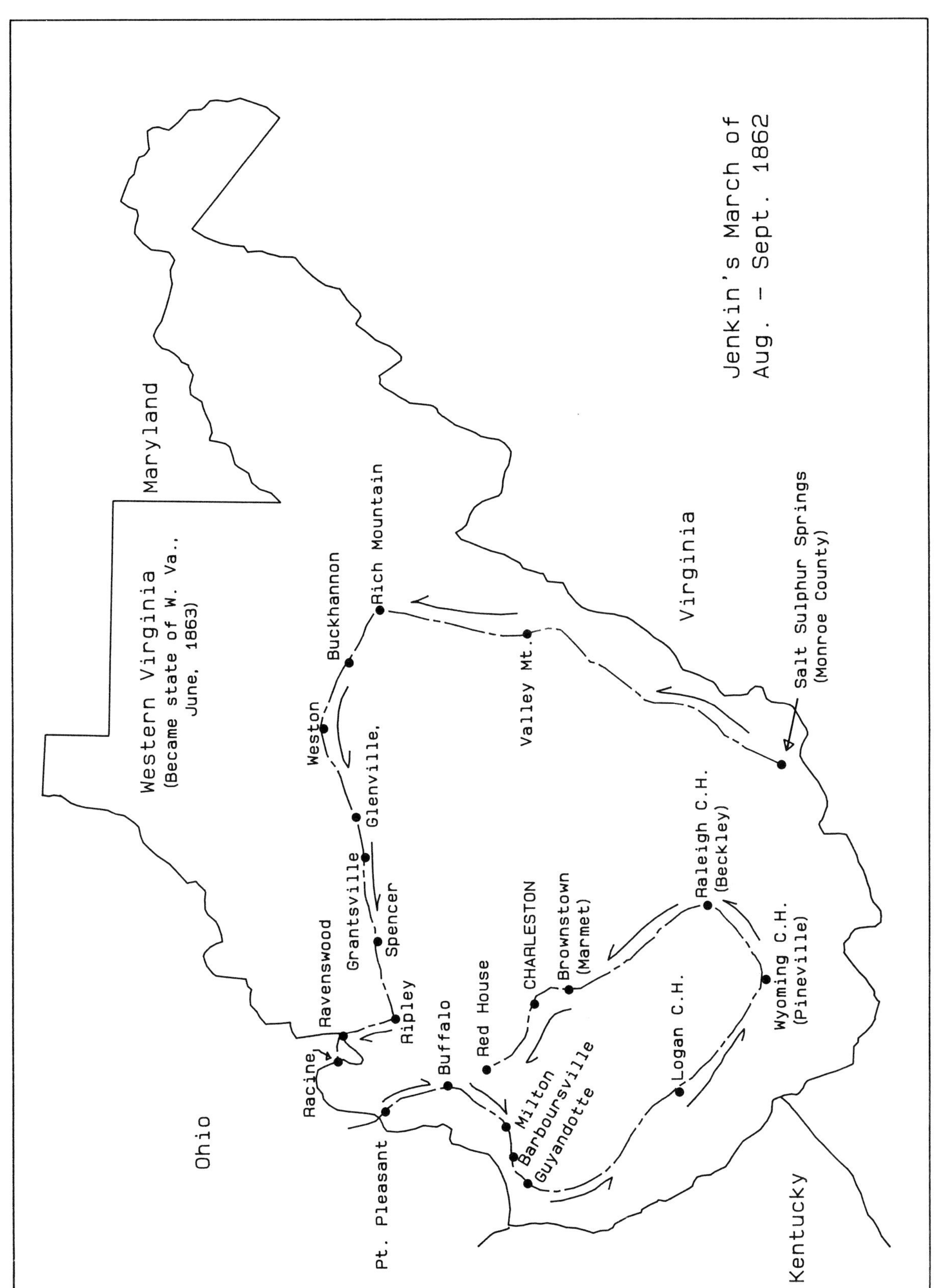

Map of West Virginia showing the route of General Jenkins and his Confederate cavalry on their famous march of Aug. and Sept. 1862. When they crossed the Ohio River at Ravenswood on Sept. 4, they became the first Confederate force to raise their flag on Ohio soil.

arms, along with ordnance stores and clothing.

Late that night, the command remounted and resumed the march. They headed for Weston, the county seat of Lewis County. The Confederates surrounded the town, but the Federals managed to escape in a dense fog. The raiding force did capture a dozen prisoners, and remained there the rest of Aug. 31. That evening, after destroying the telegraph office, the force took up the march again, this time heading for Glenville in Gilmer County. After finally going into camp about midnight, they resumed their march early the next morning and arrived near Glenville about 11 a.m. on Sept. 1. The Federals, consisting of only two companies, fled after a single volley from the Confederates.

At sunset the raiders were on the march again, this time heading for Spencer, the Roane County seat. Arriving there about 4 p.m. on Sept. 2, the Confederates surprised the Federal garrison. They captured the entire command of Col. John C. Rathbone, consisting of five companies of the 11th West Virginia Infantry. All the prisoners were given the oath and paroled. Sedinger stated that the Confederates were received by the citizens as their deliverers.

The next morning, the raiding force left for Ripley in Jackson County. On the evening of Sept. 3, Jenkins led his column into Ripley. Here the only Federal was a Union Army paymaster who was promptly relieved of $5,525 in U.S. funds.

The next morning, Sept. 4, Jenkins marched to Ravenswood on the Ohio River. The Federals there, numbering about 200, fled across the river. After resting all that day, near sunset Jenkins and his men crossed the Ohio and became the first Confederate force to raise the Confederate flag on Ohio soil.

Part of the command had been left on the Virginia side and was to effect a junction with the main body near Point Pleasant.

Forming on a little knoll at Portland, Ohio, Jenkins and a force of about 350 men rode to Racine. Racine is a few miles upriver from Pomeroy. Once at Racine, the general assured the uneasy citizens along the line of march that the Confederates were not barbarians and that they would be exempted from the "horrors of a savage warfare."

Jenkins remarked, "It was a curious and unexpected thing to hear upon the soil of Ohio shouts go up for Jeff Davis and the Southern Confederacy. This was usually in isolated spots where there were no near neighbors to play the spy and informant."

The Pomeroy "Weekly Telegraph" reported later that there were 400 Union troops in Racine who surrendered without a fight and were paroled. The arms, ammunition and stores fell into the hands of Jenkins and his men.

After rounding up approximately 25 horses, Jenkins and his force attempted to recross the Ohio River at Racine. There a Union sympathesizer attempted to drown the Confederates by leading them into deep water. Jenkins, however, realized the plot and called upon Mr. Burdett, a steamboat pilot who had helped Jenkins cross the Ohio on Sept. 4. The force moved a few miles downriver and did effect a safe crossing.

The force camped for the night and the next day made junction with their detached comrades six miles from Point Pleasant.

At Point Pleasant, Jenkins found the Federals to be barricaded in the courthouse and another building nearby. Realizing that an assault on this place would take cannon which had been abandoned as too cumbersome, Jenkins feinted at Point Pleasant with a small body of troops and then marched on to Buffalo on the Kanawha River. After occupying Buffalo, Jenkins' men crossed the Kanawha at 1 a.m. on either Sept. 6 or 7. They then marched overland until they struck the Ohio River near Greenbottom. The

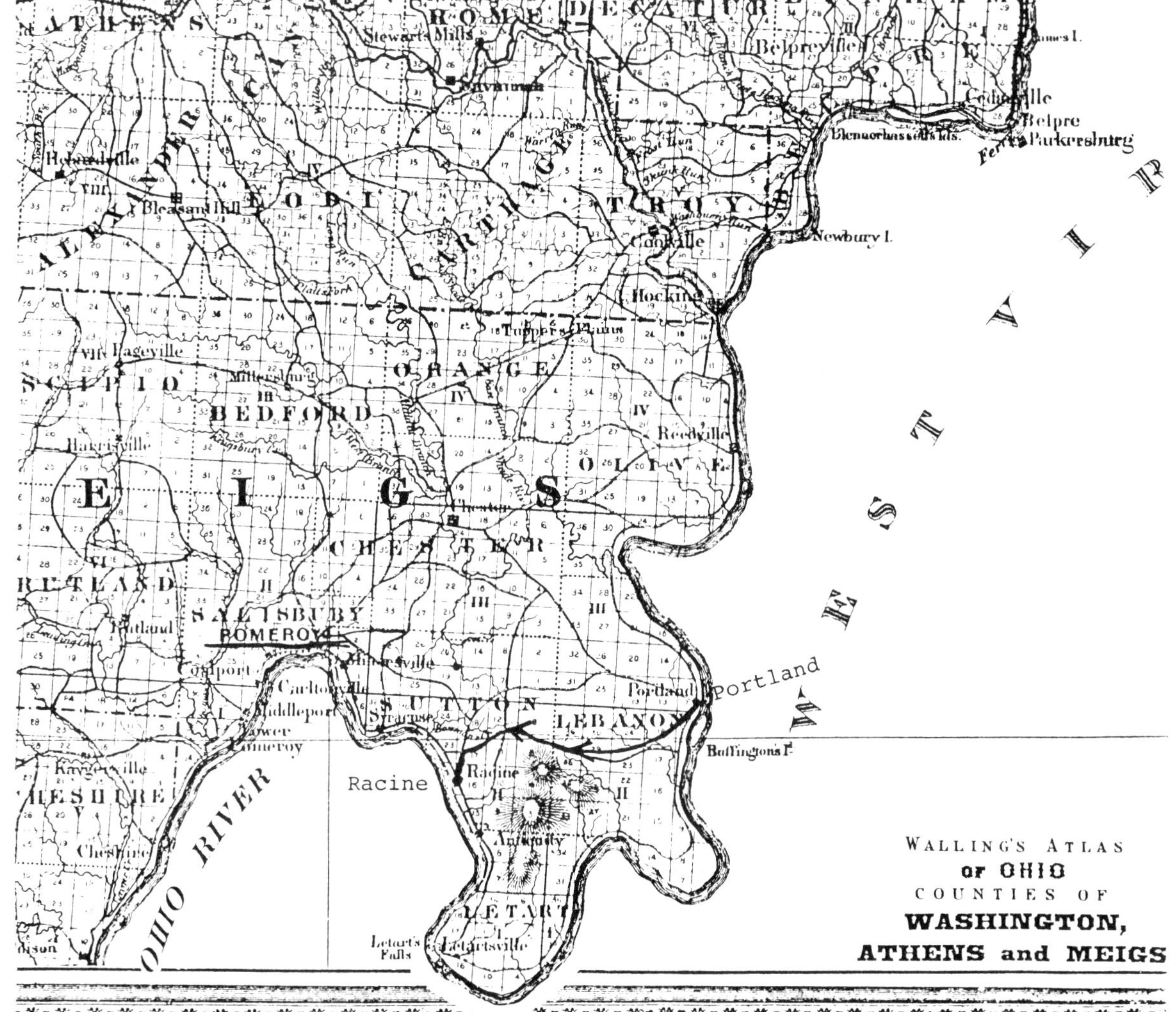

1868 map of Meigs County, Ohio, showing the route of Jenkins and his brigade after crossing into Ohio at Portland on Sept. 4, 1862.

men and their horses rested a day and a night at the Greenbottom plantation.

On Sept. 8, part of the force advanced to Barboursville where they later were joined by Jenkins. The Border Rangers took time out to visit their families and friends. The command reassembled in Barboursville, staying there two days in the event they would be needed in the rear guard action planned by General Loring.

Jenkins stated in his report that traveling with his cavalry were about 300 unarmed recruits whom he wanted to convey safely within the Confederate lines. To accomplish this, Jenkins determined to move to Logan Courthouse.

On arriving in Logan and not hearing of Loring's advance, the command was moved to Wyoming Courthouse (now Pineville.) On arriving there Jenkins heard that Loring was attacking the Kanawha Valley, and he left his command with an escort and traveled to Raleigh Courthouse (now Beckley.) Here Jenkins learned that Loring had already attacked the Union forces at Fayetteville, eight miles from the mouth of Gauley River. Jenkins rendezvoused with his command at Coal River and after a forced march down Coal River found that Loring had forced the Federals back so quickly that Jenkins and his cavalry could not get in the rear of the enemy. Here Jenkins broke off pursuit and headed for Charleston. The 500-mile raid was completed.

General Loring heaped praise upon the 32-year-old general, saying he had exhibited a policy of clemency that won the Confederates many followers and "mitigated the ferocity which had characterized the war in this section." Even though Jenkins and his men captured about 300 prisoners whom they paroled; killed, wounded, and dispersed about 1,000 of the enemy; destroyed several garrisons and 5,000 small arms; reclaimed about 40,000 square miles of territory for the Confederates, the raid went practically unrecognized by the Confederate government. This was due to the attack by Confederate Gen. Kirby Smith on Cincinnati. This raid occurred at the same time and drew national attention.

On Sept. 12, Jenkins and his force was camped somewhere in Wayne County He penned a letter to the commanding officer of the "Home Guards" of Wayne County, in which he agreed to return certain property, in exchange for the release of certain "non-combatants, heretofore arrested by you. . . ." Albert Jenkins finished the letter by giving his view of civilized warfare:

> I abhor a war on private persons and on private property, and in this I do but represent the feelings and policy of our own government. We have been compelled to pursue a different course at times as the only means of securing us against the aggressions upon the private rights and private property, which has marked the conduct of many of your military commanders.
>
> We would hail with great delight the return of your people to a more civilized mode of warfare and are ourselves ready to conform to the same in every possible respect.

Toward the end of September, part of the Jenkins command, along with Milton Ferguson's battalion of Virginia Cavalry, skirmished with the Federals at Red House Shoals in Putnam County. Jenkins probably remained with the main body of his force at Charleston.

In late October 1862, General Loring ordered a general retreat and evacuation of the Kanawha Valley. Jenkins and his cavalry were moved to Greenbrier County. Loring was then relieved of command and Gen. John Echols was appointed his successor. After reaching that area, General Lee ordered Jenkins to report for duty in the Shenandoah Valley. There his brigade became part of the "Valley Defenses." During the winter Jenkins was in charge of finding foraging sites for the cavalry horses. He appealed to his old acquaintance, Gov. Zebulon Vance of North Carolina, to help him in this effort. As a result the cavalry mounts were wintered there until spring of 1863. Jenkins also dispersed some of his brigade in one of the standard tasks of the cavalry during the Civil War: to act as a line of couriers. His couriers were to extend from the Valley to General Lee's headquarters, and were to guard the mountain passes.

General Jenkins, along with his wife and children, passed the winter at Salem, Va. There he rented five rooms for himself and his party. Jenkins made Salem his headquarters through May of the next year.

MILITARY CAREER: 1863

Near the end of 1862 the people of North Carolina complained about the foraging of the Confederate cavalry horses in their state. While the cavalrymen in charge of the horses paid the people for the forage consumed, the payment was in Confederate currency. The Carolinians often refused this payment. Therefore, on Jan. 28, 1863, General Jenkins addressed a letter to Governor Vance. In this letter, Jenkins stated:

Confederate cavalry on the march somewhere in Virginia.

In thus distributing these animals, and after overstocking almost every part of Virginia, it became a matter of necessity to send some of them to portions of North Carolina where both grain and long forage were abundant. But unfortunately, there is a great indisposition on the part of the people there to sell their produce for Confederate money at any price, and I desire to ask relief at your hands in the form of authority of some kind of impressment.

It appears that the horses did remain in that area until spring.

The cavalry units of western Virginia spent the winter months at Camp Zirkle near Salem, northwest of Roanoke. Here, in January, the 16th Virginia Cavalry was organized from six companies of Ferguson's battalion and four companies of Maj. Otis Caldwell's Battalion. Also while camped there, the 17th Virginia Cavalry was formed. General Jenkins, being the commanding officer in this area, took part in overseeing these organizations. The organization of Confederate regiments consisted of the elections of the regimental and company officers, and usually the readjusting of various company strengths. This readjusting was necessary to insure that each company had close to the 72 men required by Confederate regulations.

After the organization of the two new regiments, their muster rolls were carried to Richmond by Colonel French, the new commander of the 17th Virginia Cavalry. James A. Seddon, the Confederate secretary of war, protested that the 16th Virginia was not "perfected," on account of some of the companies not containing the requisite number of men. Jenkins then composed the following letter to Seddon. It is given here in its entirety, as its contents also speak to the importance of gathering men from the counties of western Virginia:

Hdqtrs Cavalry Brigade Army West Va
Salem, Roanoke Co. Va. Feb 8th 1863

Hon. James A. Seddon
Sec. War—
Sir-

I learn from Col. W. H. French who bore to the War Dept. the muster rolls of the companies of Col. M. J. Feguson's Regiment as well as his own, that you did not consider the former regiment perfected on account of two or three of the companies not containing the number of men required by law.

Col. Ferguson who will hand you this has had his rolls perfected by correcting this matter having transferred from the larger companies the necessary number to the smaller ones.

What I now write to request is that the appointments of the field officers of this regiment shall bear date from the 15th Jan. last that being the day upon which they were elected. I trust that this may be done. I think it is but simple justice to these officers & their regiment. Gen. Loring while in command of this department authorized me more than once to muster in companies & allow them to elect their officers, which did not have the number required by the regulations. He authorized me to use my discretion in the matter. A brief statement of the circumstances will show not only the policy but the necessity of that course. Now a body of volunteers would come from within the enemys lines in Western Virginia & propose to enlist as a company in our command, but their number perhaps would fall a few short of the required figures—how if this body of men was not received at once as a company there was no way of retaining them in the Confederate service, they being from within the enemys lines & not reached by the conscript law. If not recd at once some of them would be induced to enter the state line. Others would—off & the whole body be scattered—services lost to the Confederacy. But if then recd at once as a company, mustered into service & their officers elected, there was never the slightest difficulty in increasing their number to the maximum allowed by regulations, from their neighbors & friends who were constantly being brought out by the aid of our scouting parties and expeditions in the enemys lines. Sir, I remember rightly I mentioned this matter to you when I saw you last & explained the necessity which occasion if existed of securing a company from within the enemys lines which might fall a little short of the number required by the regulations, when I knew that the company would certainly be filled up thereafter.

Col. Fergusons Regiment now averages seventy-two rank & file to the company—and by the transfers spoken of, they are so equated that each company has the requisite number. I trust that he will have his appointment bear date from the time of his election.

Very Respectfully,
yours & c-
A. G. Jenkins
Brig. Gen'l.

The organization of the two regiments was allowed to date from the actual election of officers, as Jenkins requested. The two new regiments were placed in Jenkins' cavalry brigade.

On March 18 the first march from winter quarters began. Jenkins and a part of his brigade departed on another raid across western Virginia. This force consisted of 400 men from the 8th and 16th Virginia Regiments. Many of the men were poorly clothed or barefoot. Their target was Point Pleasant, on the Ohio River. A number of U. S. government horses and military supplies were rumored to be stored there.

Battle flag of the 8th Virginia Cavalry Regiment. Based on the Confederate "Stainless" banner, it was put into use after the battle at White Sulphur Springs on Aug. 27, 1863.
Author's collection

On March 27, Jenkins intercepted a man hauling bacon to the Federals at Hurricane Bridge. Based on information obtained from this man, Jenkins moved to Hurricane Bridge. He and his men arrived there about daylight on March 28. The small fort was commanded by Capt. James W. Johnson and part of the 13th West Virginia Infantry. Under a flag of truce, Jenkins sent in the following surrender request:

> Hurricane Bridge, Va. Mar. 28, 1863
>
> Colonel Commanding Thirteenth Regiment U. S. Volunteers,
>
> Colonel: I have now an overwhelming force so disposed as to completely surround you and cut off your retreat. A humane desire to avert the loss of life induces me to demand your surrender. In the event of your compliance, and the surrender in good faith of all forces under your command, they shall receive the treatment warranted by the usages of war, and both officers and men will be paroled. Twenty minutes will be allowed for the consideration of this note and to return a reply.
>
> I am, colonel, very respectfully, your obedient servant.
>
> A. G. Jenkins
> Brigadier-General, C.S. Army

Johnson replied that he would not surrender unless forced to by a superior number. The Confederates posted sharpshooters armed with "globe-sighted" rifles on a nearby ridge. After a siege of five hours, Jenkins determined he could not dislodge the Federals without artillery, which the Confederates had not brought with them. The Confederates marched around the fort and moved to Buffalo.

At Buffalo, the cavalry captured two flatboats and floated down the Kanawha River toward Point Pleasant.

On March 29, Jenkins and his men established a blockade on the Kanawha River, near Point Pleasant, for the purpose of capturing the steamer "Victor No. 2." This steamboat had on board a Federal paymaster with a large supply of government funds. After a sharp encounter the boat eluded the Confederates and made its way to Point Pleasant. Point Pleasant was occupied by a company of Union troops under the command of Capt. J. D. Carter. The pilot of the steamer, Capt. Frederick Ford, warned Carter and his men of the approach of the Jenkins party. Carter hurriedly moved his men into the courthouse. On March 30, Jenkins and his men occupied the town and began to fire upon the Federals in the courthouse. After exchanging gunfire for four hours, with no result on either side, reinforcements for the Federals arrived by ferry. At this point Jenkins and his force withdrew, and crossed the Kanawha River. They then marched to Howell's Mill in Cabell County, where they set up camp.

While encamped at Howell's Mill, a Union force based in Charleston moved out to cut off the Jenkins force. The Confederates received information on this movement, broke camp and marched further south into Virginia.

At this time, the cavalry brigade in western Virginia had a crucial problem: firearms. On April 15, Jenkins reported to Gen. Sam Jones that he could furnish 1,000 men for immediate service, but that only about 300 of them were armed. In late April, the Jenkins Cavalry Brigade consisted of the 8th, 14th, 16th, 17th and 19th Virginia Cavalry Regiments and the 34th, 36th and 37th Virginia Cavalry Battalions. Of these units, Jenkins reported 1,140 men and 111 officers present for duty. The total aggregrate present and absent totaled 2,656. The difference was probably accounted for by men sick or home on leave, or imprisoned.

On April 25, Virginia Jenkins gave birth to the couple's third child. The daughter was named Margaret Virginia. She was born while the Jenkins family was still rooming in Salem.

Sometime in May, the brigade picked up their horses which had been foraged in North Carolina during the winter. This rendezvous was probably in the area near Staunton.

Also in May General Lee decided to go on the offensive. If the war was taken north, the pressure on Vicksburg might be relieved. Lee also saw this as an opportunity to capture much-needed food and supplies. In prelude to this invasion, Jenkins and the cavalry brigade were ordered further into the Shenandoah Valley.

Lee had some doubts whether Jenkins was the right commander for such a cavalry mission. Gen. Samuel Jones had referred to Jenkins as a bold and gallant soldier ". . . but not a good administrative officer." Jones believed him capable of great improvement, and feared making any realignments due to the fact that " . . . many of his (Jenkins') men are his constituents, and he has been a politician . . . and still has aspirations that way."

On June 3, Lee set his army in motion northward. Longstreet's First Corps left Fredericksburg on the 3rd. Ewell's Second Corps followed the next day. Hill's Third Corps left on June 14. Stuart's cavalry did not get Lee's final orders until June 25, then disappeared for a week.

By this point in time, Jenkins and his cavalry brigade were in the Valley, near Berryville. The brigade had replenished its numbers to a strength of 1,451 present for duty. When Jackson's battery was added to the brigade later in June, brigade strength would rise to about 2,000 men.

On June 7, Lee met with Generals Jenkins and Imboden and ordered them to prepare the way for the advance of the main Confederate army into the Shenandoah Valley. Lee then gave Jenkins more specific instructions:

> I desire you to have your command ready to be concentrated at Strasburg, or Front Royal, or any point in front of either, by Wednesday, the 10th instant, with a view to cooperate with a force of infantry. Your pickets can be kept in advance as far as you deem best, toward Winchester. See to their arms, ammunition, and equipments, and make arrangements for provisions and forage. Send me all information you have about the position and strength of the enemy at Winchester, Martinsburg, Charlestown, Berryville and any other point where they may be. Keep your horses as fresh as you can and have your whole command prepared for active service

Doubts or no doubts, Lee had chosen Jenkins to lead the vanguard into enemy territory.

By Friday, June 12, Ewell had brought his corps across the mountains near Front Royal and Cederville and joined with Jenkins. Here Lee skillfully maneuvered Ewell's corps and Jenkins' cavalry so they escaped detection until they appeared directly in front of the Union defenses at Berryville. Jenkins was ordered to cooperate with Gen. Rodes in the attack on Berryville. Their goal was the capturing of Gen. Robert Milroy's Third Federal Brigade, at Berryville, and then to duplicate the effort by an attack at Martinsburg.

At Berryville on June 13, Jenkins' brigade drove in the enemy cavalry but was held up by an artillery barrage. Before Rodes could attack, the Federals evacuated Ber-

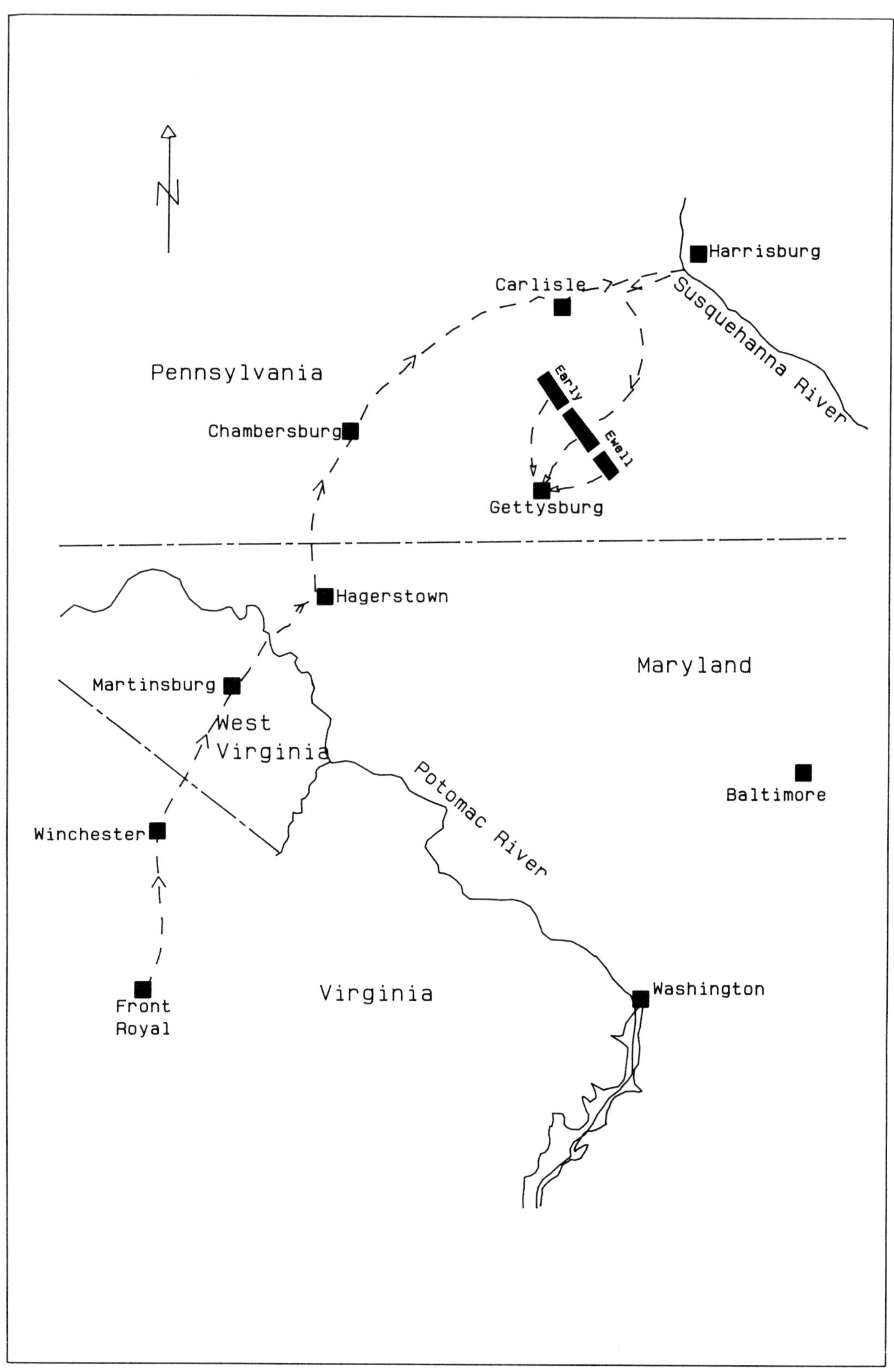

Route of Jenkins' Cavalry Brigade, June-July 1863. When the brigade halted outside of Harrisburg, PA, they attained the geographical "high-water mark" of the Confederacy.

ryville. Rodes sent Jenkins to the west of town in an effort to cut off the retreating Federals. Jenkins attacked a detachment of the Federal cavalry at Bunker Hill, where he lost several men. He did manage to capture 75 to 100 prisoners.

On the morning of June 14, Jenkins arrived in front of Martinsburg to demand that town's surrender. The demand was refused. Rodes promptly ordered Jenkins to dismount his men and move forward and endeavor to take Martinsburg. The Federals abandoned the town. Ramseur's Brigade of infantry chased the Federals northward. Jenkins, however, remounted some of his men and was able to get ahead of Ramseur. After a few rounds were fired, the Federals abandoned all of its artillery. Five Federal field pieces were captured, along with their caissons and horses. Also captured were three officers and 65 men. Jenkins continued on to the Potomac River that night. Rodes reported: "General Jenkins' gallant brigade, under his impetuous leadership, has already succeeded in crossing the Potomac above Williamsport, and after driving off the small force at that place, has advanced into Pennsylvania."

The Jenkins force moved on, and by June 15, after passing through Hagerstown, Md., came in sight of Greencastle, Pa. Here Jenkins divided his brigade into two forces. Part of the 14th Virginia Cavalry formed the right wing. This wing charged the town and the Federal cavalry escaped. After destroying the railroad depot, and cutting the telegraph wires, the brigade took up its advance to Chambersburg. Lt. Hermann Schuricht of the 14th Virginia remarked that they passed several partly burned wagons left by the Federals. At 11 o'clock that night, the Confederates entered the city of Chambersburg and went into camp.

At this point, the brigade only consisted of the 14th, 16th, and 17th Virginia Cavalry Regiments, and the 34th and 36th Battalions. The 8th and 19th Cavalry and the 37th Battalion had been split off to other commands, or left behind to act as rear guard screens.

The "Richmond Examiner" was upset over Jenkins' easy-going and soft-hearted tactics. The media expected the troopers to make the people of Pennsylvania suffer as the folks in Virginia had suffered. The newspaper wanted to see all of Franklin County (Pennsylvania) burned and devastated. Lee, on moral and psychological grounds, did not follow this method of warfare.

Some sources have stated that General Jenkins was captured around Chambersburg, and was exchanged before the battle at Gettysburg. No official records have been found to support this claim.

On June 16, 17 and 18, Jenkins and his cavalry were ordered to help the quartermasters and commissaries to obtain supplies for their departments. Although he had been carefully instructed about transacting this business by regular purchases, Jenkins did not require his men to account for large numbers of horses which they seized. To gather supplies, General Jenkins ordered the storekeepers of Chambersburg to open their establishments. The Confederates purchased what they required with Confederate money.

Since many of the people had fled the city in haste, there were many clothes and household utensils left scattered in the streets. The cavalrymen were ordered to gather up these items, and attempt to place them in the houses of their probable owners.

That night, about 9 o'clock, General Jenkins had his entire brigade alarmed, to test their readiness for action. He was very pleased with the results of the drill.

Early on the morning of the 17th, the citizens were ordered by Jenkins to give up all weapons, and about 500 guns and sabres were collected. The useful arms were loaded on wagons, and the others destroyed.

There were also rumors that the Confederates on this invasion of the north conducted searches for negroes. Supposedly those that were found were seized and sent south. Neither Lt. Schuricht nor Sedinger mentioned this in their diaries.

About mid-day on the 17th, news reached the Jenkins command that a strong Yankee force was advancing; consequently, the Confederates evacuated the city and fell back to Hagerstown, Md.

By this date, Jenkins' cavalry was still the only part of Lee's army to have reached Pennsylvania. The main force was still in Maryland.

For the next few days Jenkins detached parts of his brigade, including the 14th Virginia Cavalry, to raid the countryside and the communities of Greencastle, Waynesboro, and Fairfield. During this week, Jenkins brought the total of cattle and horses captured to 3,000 head. Some of the Jenkins raiding parties ". . . considered horses as contraband of war, and (they) were taken without the pretense of compensation."

The night of the 18th the rains started that were to plague both armies through much of the campaign.

On the 19th, Rodes' division moved northward to join Jenkins in Pennsylvania. The rest of Lee's army was still across the Potomac in Virginia or Maryland.

On Sunday, June 21, Jenkins' troops were patrolling the area between Hagerstown and Greencastle. As Jenkins rode through Greencastle he sighted two Union soldiers having their horses' shoes tightened at a blacksmith shop. They were quickly taken prisoner. Jenkins then sighted some Union cavalry on a wooded hill nearby. He moved quickly to develop an ambush. He quickly dismounted his men and sought cover in the wheatfield. After a short skirmish, resulting in one Union soldier being killed, the rest of the Union force withdrew.

On June 22, Lee addressed a letter to Gen. Ewell which showed that Lee was uncertain about the discipline and effectiveness of Jenkins' brigade. In part, he said: ". . . If necessary, send a staff officer to remain with General Jenkins." By that date the brigade was back in Chambersburg. Also the 17th Virginia Cavalry was detached and assigned to escort Gen. Jubal Early's division in a movement toward York, Pa. The Jenkins brigade was now reduced to the 14th and 16th Regiments and the 34th and 36th Battalions.

On June 23, Jenkins' chief of staff, Captain Fitzhugh, ordered the people of Chambersburg to furnish large amounts of provisions for the brigade. The provisions were to be brought to the courthouse by a specified time. Should they refuse, he stated he would institute a general search of the houses. This was the third or fourth time the Confederates had taken provisions from this group of people. Still the Confederates did obtain large amounts of goods, which they paid for in Confederate currency.

On the 24th, Robert Rodes' division finally reached Chambersburg. General Ewell himself headed the column, riding in his buggy. As the band played "The Bonnie Blue Flag," the long grey column marched through town. They were covered in dust, and many were barefoot. The infantry camped just north of town. Jenkins and his cavalry were assigned to guard the approaches from Harrisburg.

That evening, while on scout duty, Jenkins' pickets were fired upon by the a roving band of troopers. Supposedly Jenkins was pushed to near panic by this unexpected opposition. Jenkins fell back from the roads and sent for support from Chambersburg.

Ewell dispatched an infantry brigade and Jenkins' anxiety was quieted.

On June 25, the cavalry was on the move again. They moved through Shippensburg and had several minor skirmishes before they camped several miles past Shippensburg, toward Carlisle. By this date, most of Lee's army was across the Potomac and advancing toward Harrisburg.

On the 26th of June, Rodes and Johnson's divisions had joined with Jenkins and the force was now driving a large herd of confiscated cattle and a train of well-stocked provision wagons.

By June 27, the entire brigade was at Carlisle. After some skirmishing with local militia on horseback, the brigade passed the fortifications and occupied the city. By 3 p.m. Ewell's corps arrived. At this point, the town burgesses went out to meet the advancing Rebels. They stated that there were no troops in town, and implored the Confederates not to charge through the streets because of the women and children. General Jenkins said he did not want trouble and preferred to enter town as quietly as possible. As a result, the cavalry entered Main Street with their horses at a walk. However, they rode with their carbines resting on their legs in readiness if fired upon. Jenkins then demanded of the town council 1,500 rations to be furnished within the hour. Jenkins said that unless his demands were met his men would help themselves. In less than an hour the stalls of the market house were piled high with all kinds of eatables.

Jenkins camped his brigade near the century-old cavalry depot outside of town, and set up his headquarters at the barracks.

That evening Ewell and the Second Corps arrived in town. General Jenkins was ordered to proceed to the Susquehanna River and scout the approaches and defenses of Harrisburg. Ewell sent his chief engineer, H. B. Richardson, with Jenkins.

By 9 a.m. on the 28th, Jenkins and the brigade arrived at a hill some four miles outside of Harrisburg, the state capital. Here Jenkins sent Col. Ferguson with his 16th Virginia, along with the 36th Battalion and Jackson's four-gun battery, along the north road. Ferguson's force encountered a small group of infantry and a Pennsylvania battery, and after a shelling, dislodged the defenders, who fell back to a stronger position near Oyster's Point. With the remainder of the brigade Jenkins took position on the Silver Springs turnpike, a road that ran parallel to the Carlisle-Harrisburg turnpike. An artillery battle resumed, which continued until dusk. Jenkins watched the duel and decided not to attack until the next day.

On the 29th, Ewell received word from Lee's headquarters that the Second Corps was ordered immediately to Gettysburg and ordered Jenkins to leave the vicinity of Harrisburg. General Jenkins, however, did not receive the order until 2 p.m. and began moving his force late in the afternoon. Lt. Schuricht and the 14th Virginia had been within sight of the city. This marked the northernmost point reached by Confederate troops in the entire campaign. Therefore, while Gettysburg has always been spoken of philosophically as the "high water mark of the Confederacy," Albert Gallatin Jenkins and his cavalry force actually achieved the geographical high water mark.

On June 30, Jenkins ordered the 14th Virginia and Jackson's battery to proceed at once to Mechanicsburg and to hold the town. Jenkins had decided to spend the night at the home of a local merchant named Hiteshaw. On July 1, Jenkins remarked to Hiteshaw that the Army of the Potomac was still down in Virginia and that it would take weeks for it to reach Pennsylvania. He supposedly boasted that: "We expect to remain here all summer." At sunset a courier rode in and ordered the astounded Jenkins back to Carlisle. The entire command moved out and did not bivouc until 2 a.m. The men and horses received little rest after this march, as Jenkins was nervous. He feared an enemy attack and kept the men under arms and their mounts saddled.

After the war, Jenkins and his men were accused of being of little value to Ewell during the month of June. It has been stated that Gen. John Buford (U.S.A.) easily kept the less experienced troops of Jenkins from spying on the Union forces advancing south of Gettysburg. Others have stated that if the men had been guided by another cavalry leader such as Stuart, Wade Hampton, or Fitz Lee, they might have served with more purpose. Debate on this point will be left to those more experienced in military tactics.

By daybreak on July 1, the cavalry was again on the road to Gettysburg. Lt. Schuricht reported upon reaching the vicinity of Gettysburg:

> During the forenoon we heard heavy cannonading from that direction, and soon we learned that the two hostile armies had met unexpectedly. The Federal troops were finally defeated, but the loss on both sides was heavy and that of the Union army the most severe. General Reynolds, the commanding general, was among the dead, and thousands of prisoners were taken by our victorious troops.

Probably when the brigade reached Gettysburg, or the day before, the 17th Virginia Cavalry rejoined the Jenkins brigade. During the first day of the battle, half of the brigade was put in charge of guarding the 5,000 Union prisoners captured that day. The other portion of the brigade was held in reserve.

The morning of the second day of the battle brought the following, as described directly by Lt. Schuricht:

> In the morning we advanced into the valley between Seminary Ridge and the mountain range held by the Union Army. Jenkins' Brigade was posted in a piece of woodland, part of yesterday's battlefield, in sight of the seminary and the city of Gettysburg. Both armies had been reinforced and concentrated during the night. General Stuart, with the main force of our cavalry, was not at hand, and for want of cavalry the defeated Federals had not been pressed, and still held and fortified the eminence, above Gettysburg, controlling the valley. Our forces were in possession of the town. We were wondering at the silence prevalent, only in long intervals the report of a gun was heard. General Jenkins resolved to reconnoitre, and I was of his companions. Arrived on top of a hill our party attracted the enemy's attention, and we were fired upon. A shell exploded among us, wounding the General and his horse. The hours dragged on wearily, until in the afternoon twenty-seven Confederate batteries opened fire on the enemy's lines.

After the wounding of General Jenkins, Col. Milton J. Ferguson of the 16th Virginia Cavalry assumed command of the brigade. The men fought well the next day, even though they were supplied with only ten rounds of ammunition for their Enfield rifles. This supply, which had been put into effect while on the scouting mission in late June, had never been increased due to an oversight. Therefore they had to withdraw from the field early in the afternoon of July 3.

There is little else known about the wounding of Albert Jenkins on July 2, 1863. An account in the "Southern Illustrated News" of Oct. 3 stated that Jenkins was

> . . . standing near the battlefield of Gettysburg, holding his horse by the bridle with one hand and with the other holding up a map of the surrounding country, which he was gazing intently upon, a shell from the enemy's lines exploded in close proximity, killing his horse and severly wounding him in the head.

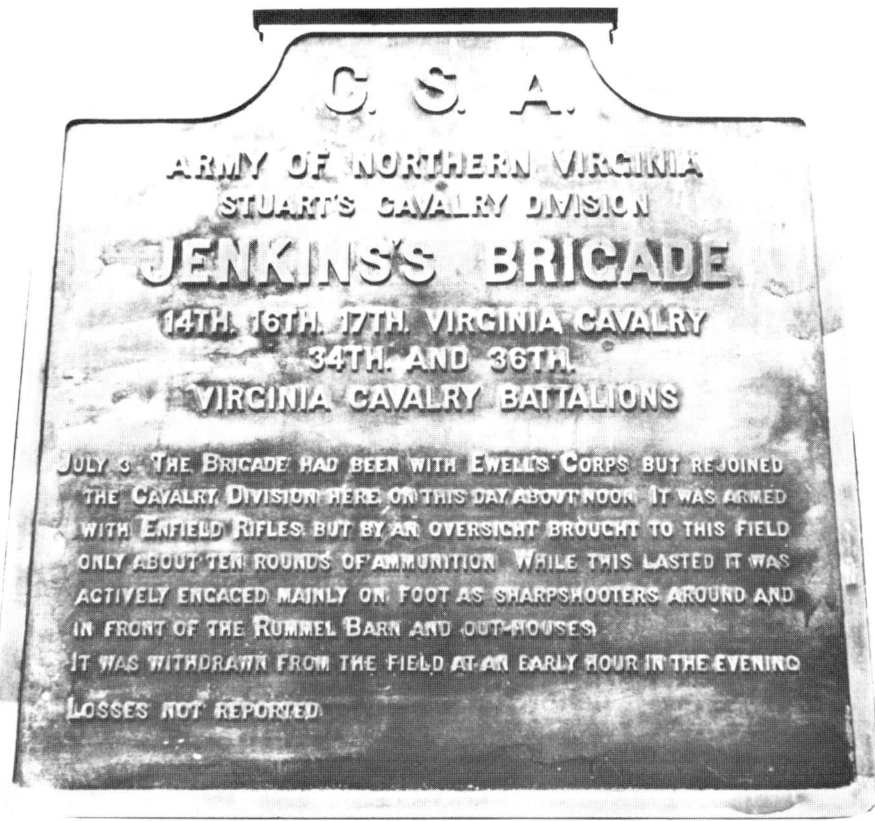

The Jenkins Brigade marker in the East Cavalry Field, Gettysburg National Battlefield Park. Author's collection

The general was evidently carried to a house in the town, to be cared for by Confederate surgeons. The next mention is on July 4, when Lt. Schuricht stated that he passed by the house where the wounded general was quartered. There he inquired about the general's health, and asked if Gettysburg was still in Confederate hands. The only recorded response to this inquiry was that the general's adjutant laughed at the lieutenant's doubt. (This adjutant was probably James P. Whitman of the 16th Virginia Cavalry.) That same day, after some artillery fire near this house, Schuricht stated that the adjutant hastened to remove "our general" to some place of safety.

Immediately following the battle, General Rodes mentioned Jenkins and eight others in his report as having won distinction in the Gettysburg campaign.

The next few months are sketchy to say the least. Sources disagree widely on how long Albert Jenkins was out of action as a result of his head wound. Douglas S. Freeman stated that Jenkins was one of the six Confederate generals who was back in command in a few weeks following Gettysburg. Other sources state it was the fall of 1863 before Jenkins was back in action.

Harrisonburg Va Aug 5 1863

Hon James A Seddon
Secretary of War
Sir

I hereby tender my resignation as Brig. Genl (Cavalry) P. A. C. S. on account of a recent sad affliction in my family which renders my presence with them necessary.

My wife has lost the use of both eyes, with but little hope of even the ultimate restoration of vision-

I remain
Very Respy yours
A. G. Jenkins
Brig. Genl. Cav.

Through
Major Genl Stuart

A copy of General Jenkins' resignation, dated Aug. 5, 1863. The last paragraph states: "My wife has lost the use of both eyes, with but little hope of . . . the ultimate restoration of vision." Robert E. Lee refused its acceptance, as he had no one to appoint in his place.

Jenkins was well enough on July 7 to sign a requisition for forage for four horses kept at Winchester. It is doubtful that Jenkins was actually in Winchester at the time, as the main Confederate Army did not retreat across the Potomac River until July 12.

From the article published in the "Southern Illustrated News," we know that Jenkins did recuperate in Lexington, Va., for some weeks following his wounding. The newspaper article described him as being:

> . . . about five feet ten inches high, well formed and of good physique; dark hair, blue eyes, and heavy brown beard; pleasing countenance, kind, affable manners, fluent and winning in conversation; quick, subtle and argumentative in debate.

On Aug. 5, General Jenkins was in Harrisonburg and penned a short letter to James A. Seddon, Confederate secretary of war. In this letter he tendered his resignation due to a ". . . recent sad affliction in my family." He went on to state that his wife had lost the use of both eyes, with little hope of ever recovering her vision. On the back of this letter Gen. Stuart recommended its acceptance as Jenkins (in his opinion) was not a good disciplinarian. Stuart hoped that a good disciplinarian and more experienced officer would be appointed in his place. Gen. Lee responded that he could not recommend its acceptance as he had no one else to appoint in his place.

By September, however, the movement was on again to have Jenkins promoted. A petition signed by 32 men from western Virginia and West Virginia was sent to Seddon on Sept. 22, recommending Jenkins for promotion to the rank of major general. The petition was not received until October, and was marked by Seddon as: "File for consideration when there is a division to which an appointment can be made . . ."

Lee was now convinced that the existing cavalry brigades in his army were too large. He reduced all the brigades and legions to smaller units. Jenkins' brigade was reduced officially to three regiments and two battalions. On Oct. 31, Brig. Gen. Jenkins was still shown as the brigade commander.

The brigade was detached from Stuart's command, and moved down the Shenandoah Valley further into Virginia. They were near Lewisburg in late September. In November the brigade was again reduced. This time the Jenkins brigade was to consist of only the 14th, 16th and 17th Virginia Cavalry Regiments. On Nov. 30, 1863, Col. Milton J. Ferguson of the 16th Virginia was shown as commanding the brigade.

As winter approached, Jenkins probably sent the horses further south again for winter forage.

MILITARY CAREER: 1864

It is possible that during the winter of 1863-64 a fourth child was born to Albert and Virginia. Tradition has held that this last child was named George.

In early January 1864, Albert G. Jenkins and his brigade moved up the Shenandoah Valley to Woodstock to prepare for a raid on the Baltimore & Ohio Railroad. On February 11 he was organizing and recruiting a large cavalry corps to be used in western Virginia (and West Virginia) in the coming spring. At that time the brigade was in camp at the narrows of the New River in Giles County. From there Jenkins moved his men to Callaghan's Station near Covington, Va. They arrived in that area about Feb. 21. On Feb. 24 the brigade was at Franklin, with Gen. Echols and the cavalry of Col. W. L.

Jackson and Gen. John Imboden.

The condition of the men in the brigade was poor by this point in the war. Clothing and shoes were sorely needed. Medical facilities were very good despite an outbreak of chicken pox. The men were armed with .54- and .58-caliber Enfield and Austrian rifles. Each man had about 40 rounds of ammunition.

The Confederacy then established the Department of Southwestern Virginia. On Feb. 25 Maj. Gen. John C. Breckinridge was placed in command of the approximately 7,000 troops in the department, which included Jenkins' brigade. Jenkins' cavalry brigade was shown as being composed of the 14th, 16th, 17th and 22nd Regiments. General Jenkins was shown as the brigade commander.

By the end of March, the 17th Cavalry was detached and temporarily assigned to another command. The remainder of the Jenkins' brigade was encamped back at Callaghan's Station.

In April General Jenkins took a short leave to visit his family. This leave was extended by the Adjutant & Inspector General's Office to at least April 19. By the end of April, the 17th Cavalry had rejoined the Jenkins brigade. Now under Jenkins were the same four regiments as on Feb. 25.

As Union Gen. Franz Sigel moved down the Valley toward Stuanton, Lee requested help from Breckinridge. Breckinridge sent 4,000 of his infantry and 12 pieces of artillery on a train from Staunton. The defense of the Trans-Allegheny was left to Brig. Gen. Jenkins and his brigade. Breckinridge sent Jenkins a message reading: "You see the whole country west of new River is uncovered and depends on you."

Probably in late April, Jenkins was appointed cavalry commander of the Department of Western Virginia with headquarters at Dublin.

THE FINAL BATTLE: May 1864

In the early days of May 1864, a Federal force under Gen. George Crook was moving to attack the Virginia & Tennessee Railroad and destroy the Confederate stores at Dublin. His force consisted of the 9th and 14th West Virginia Infantry, the 7th West Virginia Cavalry, the 23rd, 36th, 12th, 91st and part of the 34th Ohio Infantry, a reserve brigade of the 3rd and 4th Pennsylvania Reserves, and the 11th and 15th West Virginia Vol. Infantry, along with two artillery batteries. His force, consisting of about 6,000 men, departed Charleston on May 2. Crook moved through Fayetteville and Princeton and on to the area of Cloyd's Mountain in Pulaski County, Va.

Col. John McCausland's Confederate brigade consisted of the 36th Virginia Infantry, Lt. Col. Thomas A. Smith commanding, and the 60th Virginia Infantry, Col. Beuhring H. Jones commanding, and the 45th Battalion Virginia Infantry, Lt. Col. Henry Beckley commanding. This brigade had spent the winter of 1863-64 near Princeton, Mercer County, W.Va. About the 1st of May this Confederate force fell back to Dublin Depot on the Virginia & Tennessee Railroad and was joined by the 45th Virginia Infantry, Lt. Col. Harman commanding. The 45th had spent the winter in Bland County, Va. Also joining the Confederate force were three artillery batteries: Bryan's Battery, the Ringgold Battery, and Douthat's Botetourt Artillery. In addition, the Southern force was reinforced by the Montgomery County Home Guard under Capt. White G. Ryan. The entire command totaled about 3,000 men.

McCausland moved his brigade behind some rifle pits and barriers of inverted

Gen. George Crook, USA. He was in command of Union forces at the battle of Cloyd's Mountain. It was one of Crook's soldiers who wounded Jenkins.

fence rails that had been constructed near the base of Cloyd's Mountain. In front of these were earthworks, and the Confederate artillery was in a strategic position behind the earthworks.

Brig. Gen. Albert G. Jenkins arrived during the evening of May 8 and assumed command of the Confederate force, being the senior officer. He established his headquarters at "Back Creek," the residence of James M. Cloyd.

It was not until the morning of May 9, 1864, that the 45th Virginia Infantry arrived. Jenkins at this point changed the original position of the Confederate line. McCausland voiced his objections to this change, which went unheeded. James Cloyd, the owner of the farm, also expressed his objections. Jenkins supposedly remarked that Cloyd was a planter and not knowledgeable in military matters. Military strategists have stated that this stretched parts of the Confederate line too thin and left other parts exposed to a flank attack.

About 9 a.m. the Confederate pickets on the summit of the mountain were driven in. Crook's infantry was seen advancing along a bridle path leading toward the mountain, with his right wing resting upon the pike—the same spot upon which rested the Confederate left.

The battle was in full force by 10:30 and raged unabated until 12:30, when Jenkins ordered a charge by the 45th Regiment and Beckley's battalion. This attack did result in breaking the Federal line, but the charge was checked and turned by the second line of Federal troops. The 36th Virginia, lying on the left, was then ordered to charge, but was also stopped. As he was riding back and forth with upraised sword, trying to rally the charge, a musket ball shattered the left arm of General Jenkins and he was borne from the field.

Historical marker located in a field just outside of Dublin, VA.

The Federals in turn charged, with the 9th West Virginia in the lead. The Confederate lines broke and the entire force was soon in full retreat toward Dublin Depot, with the cavalry in pursuit. The day before, Gen. John Hunt Morgan had routed Union General Averill at Wytheville. Five hundred of Morgan's 5th Kentucky Cavalry, leaving their horses at Wytheville, came by train to Dublin Depot. There they detrained and started for the scene of the battle, and when one mile and a half out met and temporarily checked the Federal advance. This allowed the retreating Confederates to regroup at New River Bridge. Thus began and ended the bloodiest battle ever fought in southwestern Virginia. The Confederates lost heavily in officers. In addition to Jenkins, Maj. George W. Hammond, Maj. Jacob Taylor, and Captain McClintic, all of the 60th Virginia, and Lt. Col. Edwin H. Harman of the 45th Virginia were mortally wounded. Total Confederate losses were given as: 76 killed, 262 wounded, and 200 missing or captured. Crook's losses were given as: 108 killed, 508 wounded, and 72 missing or captured.

Jenkins, along with Maj. Thomas L. Broun and Lt. Col. Thomas Smith, were taken to the nearby John Guthrie home instead of the field hospital which the Federals had set up. The Guthrie home was one of two appropriated by the Federals to care for

The John Guthrie home near Cloyd's Mountain, Pulaski County, VA as it appears today. Gen. Albert G. Jenkins was brought here after he was wounded May 9, 1864.
Author's collection

some of the wounded Confederate officers. Five surgeons were detailed by the Federal medical director to stay with the wounded, while the main Union force moved on in pursuit of the retreating Confederates. Dr. N. F. Graham of the 12th Ohio Infantry was in charge. The other doctors were: Dr. William S. Newton of the 91st Ohio, Walsh and Johnston of the 15th West Virginia, and Dr. Thatcher of the 14th West Virginia. According to Newton, the federal surgeons stayed at Cloyd's Mountain for three weeks. Three days after the battle they were surrounded and captured by John Hunt Morgan's Kentucky Cavalry. On Thursday evening, May 12, Confederate Surgeon Watkins of the 36th Virginia came and requested that Newton visit General Jenkins. Newton stated in a letter that after seeing the general, ". . . we counseled amputation at the shoulder as the only chance for life." On the morning of the 13th the Federal surgeons were again requested to visit and amputate General Jenkins' arm. When ready to leave, however, they found that Morgan's men had confiscated their medical instruments. On learning of their intended errand, the instruments were immediately returned. The operation was successfully accomplished by Dr. N. F. Graham of the 12th Ohio Regiment, with Jenkins under the influence of chloroform. A young son of the Guthrie family and a Negro boy took the limb in a sheet and buried it in the orchard. According to Newton, Jenkins expressed much gratitude for the service and assured the surgeons of every assistance in his power in getting through the lines. Jenkins even penned a letter to James Seddon, Confederate secretary of war, attempting to get safe passage for the surgeons, but to no avail. They were sent to Libby Prison in Richmond, but were only held for three days before being exchanged.

U.S.A.

H. Qrs 3 Divi Dept W Va
Near Dublin Depot Va
May 10th 1864

I A. G. Jenkins Brig Gen. C.S.A. do solemnly declare that I will observe each and all of the stipulations hereinafter given in this my parole

1st
That I will report in person to the Officer Comdg the United States Forces at Charleston W Va as soon as I am able to travel

2d In the meantime I am not duly exchanged

A. G. Jenkins
Brig Gen C.S.A.

Witness
James Allen
Capt. 2 W V Cav
Pro Mar 3d Divi
D W Va

Albert G. Jenkins' parole, signed and dated the day after his wounding at Cloyd's Mountain. Courtesy: National Archives

Sketch by a witness of the Battle of Cloyd's Mountain. The Federals in the middle foreground are preparing to attack the Confederate defenses on the slopes in the background. Sketched by J. W. Oswald.

Following the amputation, Jenkins was supposedly attended by his wife, Virginia, as well as the Guthrie daughters, who were acting as nurses for the wounded.

On May 10, the day after his wounding, Jenkins signed his parole stating that he would report in person to the Union officer commanding forces at Charleston, W.Va., as soon as he was able to travel. This was witnessed by Capt. James Allen of the 2nd West Virginia Cavalry. This parole, along with that of Lt. Col. Thomas Smith and Lt. Col. Benjamin R. Linkous, both of the 36th Virginia, were sent to the Federal commander at Charleston. The cover letter with them, signed by Gen. Crook, stated all three ". . . were severly wounded on the 9th instant in the battle of Cloyd Mountain."

Jenkins' condition took a sudden turn for the worse, however. On the morning of the 21st a secondary hemorrhage took place. One possible cause for this has been suggested. It seems possible that a ligature which was being used to pinch off a main artery was accidently knocked loose, which caused the hemorrhage. Newton and another surgeon were sent for at 2 a.m.; they arrived at the Guthrie home an hour later, but Gen. Jenkins was already dead by that time. Newton stated: ". . . having died only a few minutes" before their arrival. Newton related in his letter: ". . . the General was a true gentleman, and had treated us with kindness. Indeed his whole command seemed willing to make our stay comfortable, and we were well pleased when this force acted as our guard."

After the death of Jenkins, the makeshift hospitals were dismantled and the Federals prepared to move on. The spoils of war taken from the wounded were collected. Colonel Rutherford B. Hayes of the 23rd Ohio (later a U.S. President) noted in a letter home that he had both the spurs of General Jenkins and the revolver belonging to Lt. Col. Thomas Smith of the 36th Virginia.

Supposedly at the time of Jenkins' wounding, he was carrying a map of the area and passed it, complete with his own bloodstains, to McCausland, who assumed command of the Confederate brigade. McCausland conducted the subsequent retreat in a skillful and brave manner and was promoted to brigadier general, to date from May 18, 1864.

There have been stories passed down regarding a certain degree of animosity between McCausland and Jenkins. John McCausland had graduated from Virginia Military Institute in 1857 and had commanded a detachment of cadets before the war. He had considered himself more qualified to be promoted to the rank of brigadier general than Jenkins, who rose in rank at least partly due to political influence and speaking ability.

Jenkins and some of the other casualties of the battle were buried in Dublin Chapel Cemetery. Here his body remained until after the end of the war. On Feb. 15, 1866, his body was moved and reinterred beside his father and mother in the family

UNION FORCES AT CLOYD'S MOUNTAIN

CONFEDERATE FORCES AT CLOYD'S MOUNTAIN

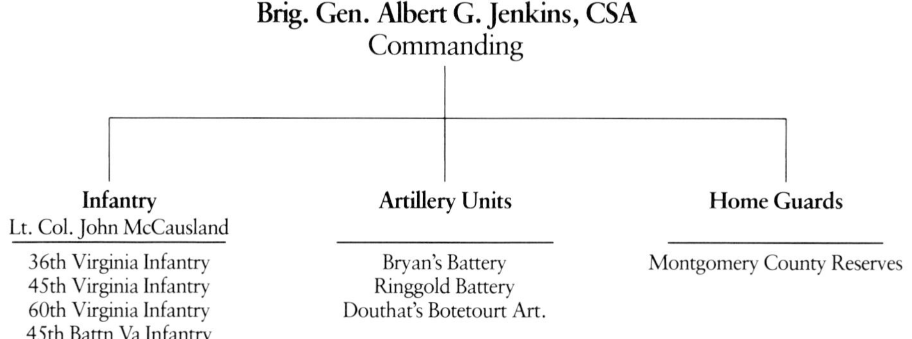

cemetery at Greenbottom.

Still not allowed to rest, Jenkins was again reinterred in the Confederate plot in Spring Hill Cemetery in Huntington, W. Va. James D. Sedinger, who had been a second lieutenant in Co. E of the 8th Virginia Cavalry, was made chairman of a committee for Camp Garnett, United Confederate Veterans, to move the body from Greenbottom to Spring Hill. At the Camp Garnett meeting held on Jan. 2, 1892, Sedinger reported that the body had been moved and that the cost had been $14.50, against which $14.00 had been raised.

Following the death of Jenkins, many of his friends and acquaintances penned beautiful words about the man and the general. James Longstreet, a Confederate lieutenant general at the time of the Battle of Cloyd's Mountain, said the following:

> In a moment of highest earthly hope he was transported to serenest heavenly joy; to that life beyond which knows no bugle call, beat of drum, or clash of steel. May his beautiful spirit, through the mercy of God, rest in peace! Amen!

In recent decades there has been a debate concerning the object of Gen. Longstreet's eulogy. Some maintain that the comments were for Gen. Micah Jenkins, another Confederate general who fell in the same month as Albert Jenkins.

The following poem, written several years after the war, is also worthy to be included as a tribute to Albert Gallatin Jenkins. It was written by Mr. T. B. Summers of Milton, Cabell County, W. Va.

Cabell County's Hero
by
T. B. Summers

Where the Ohio gently flows,
Lived a man, as history knows,
    Full of life, and at his ease,
    Yet he chose to give up these,
And bestir himself in might,
Planning for the seeming fight,
    That was hovering o'er the land,
    Seeming Peace could not command.

Wild the tempest of the day,
Telling of the coming fray,
    When the sons of North and South
    Would each face the cannon's mouth.
In the Blue, or in the Gray,
As the surge held forth its sway;
    Then no heart should fail to swear
    Both to do and bravely dare.

Then four years of strife and strain,
Brave old heroes without stain.
    Back again to friends and home,
    But so many could not come;
In the battle, they were slain,
So could never come again,
    By Ohio's rippling shore,
    Gen. Jenkins walks no more.

Jenkins Hall on the campus of Marshall University in Huntington, W.Va. It was dedicated as the Jenkins Training School for teachers on April 6, 1938. It now serves as the offices of the College of Education. Courtesy: Morrow Library, Marshall University

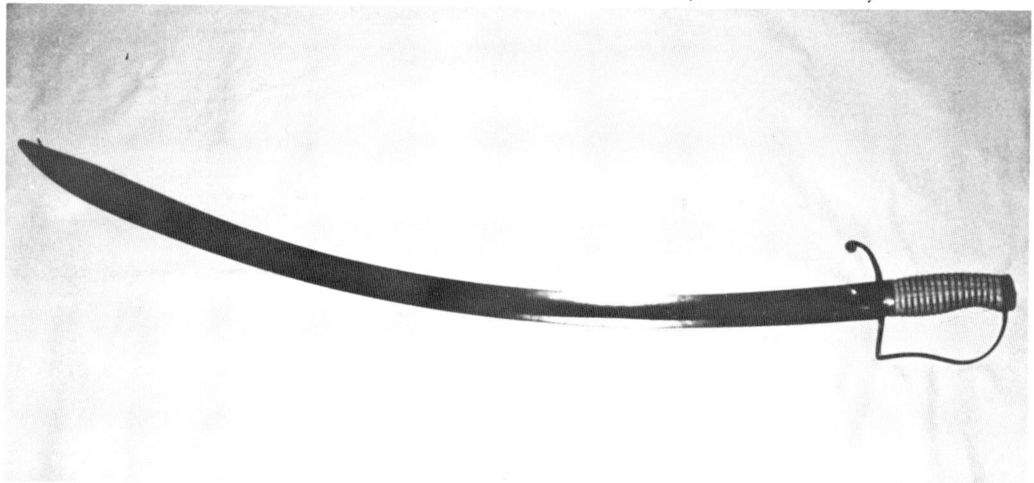

One of two swords known to have belonged to Gen. Albert G. Jenkins. The long curved blade is typical of cavalry sabers used by both sides during the war. Courtesy: Jeff Guinn

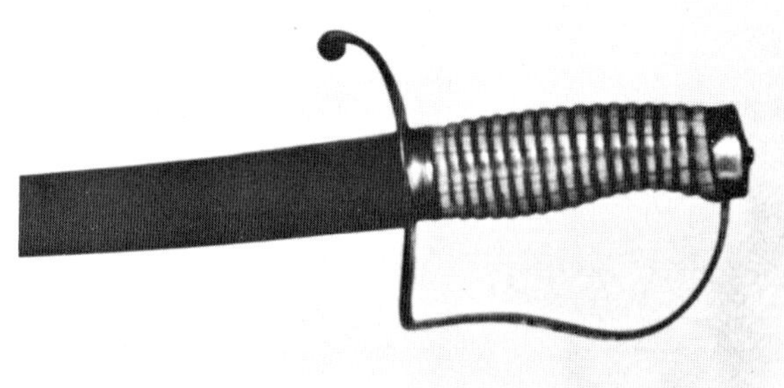

Close-up of the detail of the handle of the Jenkins sword. The ridged grip, which prevented the saber from slipping out of the officer's hand, was also typical of cavalry sabers. Courtesy: Jeff Guinn

CHAPTER SEVEN

THE ESTATE DISPUTE

EVEN BEFORE THE DEATH OF ALBERT GALLATIN JENKINS, THE DISPUTE and dismemberment of the Jenkins estate began. It should be remembered that upon the death of Capt. William A. Jenkins, the Greenbottom estate was bequeathed in three equal portions to his sons. Each received roughly 1465 acres. Property in Ironton and Cincinnati, Ohio, was also inherited by the three men.

Albert G. Jenkins along with his brothers, William A. Jenkins and Thomas J. Jenkins, inherited a valuable business block in the town of Ironton, Ohio, from their father. This block extended from the south corner of Railroad and Second Street, and was known as part of the "Rodger's Block." It was originally mortgaged by H. C. Rodgers and wife to Capt. William Jenkins in 1855. It was afterwards sold and conveyed under order of the court of Lawrence County to William Jenkins. On Nov. 3, 1860, Albert G. Jenkins bought his brothers' shares for the sum of $1.00. This deed also mentioned a tract in the town of Cincinnati on Fifth and John Streets. Margaret Virginia Jenkins, daughter of Albert G., later recalled that Albert endeavored to travel by boat down the Ohio River to Ironton after his father's death. Supposedly the people of that town would not allow his boat to land. She stated that: ". . . there was property involved—and lost." The Ironton block was seized by the U. S. authorities under the Confiscation Act of 1861. This act allowed for ". . . immediate forfeiture to the U. S. of all property of officers of the Confederate Government without warning and a similar forfeiture after 60 days warning in case of all other persons who supported the rebellion." Apparently the Cincinnati block was not seized, as the heirs of Albert G. Jenkins all were due money from this property after the war. The Cincinnati property was mentioned in various estate documents on file in Cabell County.

George S. Wallace and others state that at the November1862 term, the Cabell County grand jury returned misdemeanor indictments against A. G. Jenkins, Thomas J. Jenkins, George S. Holderby, John Clarkson, and others. No official records of these charges exist in Cabell County records, but since these men were all Confederate Army officers, it has been assumed that the indictments grew out of some of their military raids throughout the county.

On Feb. 1, 1864, Armstrong and Rice, businessmen from Ravenswood, W.Va., brought suit against Albert G. Jenkins, Thomas J. Jenkins and Nicholas Fitzhugh. (Nicholas Fitzhugh had been a lawyer from Charleston, a lieutenant in the 22nd Virginia Infantry CSA, and a friend of Albert Jenkins.) The original suit was filed in Jackson County Court, and then recorded in Cabell County. The defendants were accused of forcing, breaking and destroying three doors and locks in a store house ". . . in the town of Ravenswood, Jackson County" on Sept. 4, 1862. They were further accused of breaking and destroying: 15 iron safe boxes, 200 kegs of nails, 100 bolts of cotton, $500 worth of groceries, and other items. They were accused of "taking and carrying away" 200 bolts of calico, 100 kegs of nails, ". . . large lot of farming implements, groceries, hardware, goods and chattels to wit value of $2000." A reference to the chapter on Albert G. Jenkins' military career of 1862 will show that Sept. 4, 1862, was indeed the day that the Jenkins raiding party passed through the town of Ravenswood. As a result of this suit, there was a sale ordered on Feb. 1, 1864:

> . . . on 1465 acres of land lying on the Ohio River in Green Bottom, Cabell County, W.Va., as the property of A. G. Jenkins also 1465 acres adjoining the above as property of T. J. Jenkins being the same lands conveyed to said A. G. Jenkins and T. J. Jenkins by the late Wm Jenkins as their portion of the Greenbottom farms, also 256 acres of land on the Ohio River and on 6000 feet of land near Guyandotte also 2 acres of land near same place in Cabell County as property of T. J. Jenkins. Ordered that the sheriff of this county proceed to sell at the front door of the court house of Jackson County the property so attached.

The execution papers were dated July 19, 1864, and stated that the said A. G. Jenkins and T. J. Jenkins and Nicholas Fitzhugh were convicted. A summons, attachment, and declaration were filed during the same months.

On Aug. 15, 1864, Matthew Thompson brought suit against John Clarkson, Thomas J. Jenkins, William A. Jenkins, and others for ". . . trespass and damages of $20,000 for false imprisonment of said plantiff . . . for attachment of property of the defendants."

Also in 1864, several others brought suits against the same group of men, and also levied attachments on the lands of the Jenkins brothers. Notice was served upon the defendants in these last three cases by an article published in the Point Pleasant newspaper. In these last cases, the jury returned a verdict in favor of the plantiffs for $30,000.

Then, with the war finally over, the Reconstruction Period was not kind to ex-Confederate officers. Since West Virginia was admitted to the Union upon its creation in 1863, that state really did not go through a reconstruction period. People will be people, however, so there was animosity against the ex-Confederates in Cabell County. This lingering animosity was demonstrated in the years following the Civil War. This persecution finally ended about 1871 with the passage of the Flick Amendment, which restored the right to vote to men who had participated in the rebellion.

On Jan. 8, 1870, the lands of Thomas J. Jenkins and William A. Jenkins were ordered sold to satisfy these judgments. Later the defendants appealed, but were not allowed to plead as they could not take the "test oath." (By taking this oath, the person swore he had not held arms against the United States in the Civil War.) They appealed to the Supreme Court, which finally did find that the test oath was unconstitutional and permitted the defendants to plead.

On Sept. 10, 1866, James B. Bowlin was appointed administrator of the estate of Albert G. Jenkins. His bond was in the amount of $5,000, and one of his sureties was Albert Laidley.

On March 4, 1867, the appraisement of the estate of Albert G. Jenkins was submitted to the Cabell County Court. Enumerated in his personal property were several hundred books which Jenkins collected during his college, law school, and congressional sessions. They included the following: Shakespeare, Plutarch, Talleyrand, Longfellow, Byron, Bacon, *Roman Antiquities, Political Justice, Works of Dryden,* Botany, Philosophy, *Greek Grammar, History of Greece, History of France, Life of George Washington,* 176 volumes of Congressional documents, and 28 Blackwood's Magazines. His total personal property at Greenbottom was valued at only $1,674.

In May and June of 1867, James B. Bowlin, appearing as administrator of the estate, filed as the agent for Virginia S. Jenkins, widow; James B. Jenkins, Alberta Jenkins, and Margaret V. Jenkins, ". . . infant heirs of Albert G. Jenkins, deceased." He applied to the Board of Supervisors of Cabell County ". . . for redress against the erroneously high assessment of the lands of said widow and heirs, and to have same corrected. . . ." He stated that the previous assessment of the lands was in the amount of $35,687.40, and that it was increased to upward of $91,664.00 or equal to a 158 per cent increase. Bowlin filed similar petitions as attorney for William A. Jenkins and Thomas J. Jenkins. One of the statements showed that James B. Bowlin was residing upon the estate of A. G. Jenkins. The court did order the alterations to the land books, revaluing the real estate back to its previous assessment.

Evidently in March of 1871, the widow filed suit against the children for her right in the estate. Virginia Bowlin Jenkins had married George C. Brown in 1869. Brown had been a northern newspaper correspondent during the war. This marriage evidently caused much strife between the widow and the Jenkins children. At this time Virginia Brown was living in Hamilton County, Ohio, ". . . seperate from her husband." It was ordered in the case that "Virginia S. Brown has dower right in the estate of Albert G. Jenkins, deceased."

Also in 1871, Virginia S. Brown filed in writing her objection to the Cabell commissioners for making the lease from A. G. Jenkins to J. B. Bowlin (dated 1862) as the basis for valuation for the Greenbottom farm.

On Sept. 7, 1889, Margaret Virginia Jenkins deeded to Edmund Kyle her share in the Jenkins estate. It was stated that she owed Kyle $7,500, and had paid him $3,500 to that date. Excluded from these transfers was ". . . 1/2 acre of land which Gen. A. G. Jenkins grave is the center to remain under control of the lineal heirs of Albert G. Jenkins with right of passage." This 1/2 acre was meant to include the Jenkins family cemetery where William and Jeannette Jenkins were also buried.

In August 1910, F. A. Macdonald and Willie B. Macdonald, husband and wife, and Elliott Northcott and Lola B. Northcott, husband and wife, and Andrew J. Beardsley all deeded to Margaret Virginia Jenkins, for the sum of $20, the Jenkins family cemetery at Greenbottom.

The final blows came with a case in Cabell County Circuit Court dated Jan. 8, 1920. This case is filed as M. V. Jenkins vs. Elliott Northcott, et al. The result of this suit was the ejectment of Margaret Virginia Jenkins, and ordering that a deed, dated May 21, 1931, be written to convey the Greenbottom estate to Lola B. Northcott and Elliott Northcott. The deed, recorded in Trust Deed Book No. 266, page 546, stated that the tract contained 155.26 acres. As a result of the surveys ordered at the start of this suit, Margaret Virginia brought suit against the Northcotts for trespass. Evidently this countersuit was not continued or was thrown out.

So in the early 1930s, the last Jenkins was forced off the estate that Capt. William Jenkins had worked so hard to build up, over a hundred years before. As if to remove the last remnant of the Jenkins name from Greenbottom, Margaret Virginia had the remaining graves of her family moved from the family cemetery to Spring Hill Cemetery in Huntington. This she completed only one month before her death in 1940. Fortunately the brick mansion remains at Greenbottom, as a monument to this proud family.

Appendix

CHILDREN OF ALBERT GALLATIN JENKINS

There are records of only four children being born to the marriage of Albert G. Jenkins and Virginia S. Bowlin. They are listed here in order of their birth.

James Bowlin Jenkins:

The first child of Albert and Virginia was born Jan. 29, 1860, in Washington, D.C. He was born while Albert was serving in Congress. As a small child James traveled with his mother after the Civil War had started. They spent some time in the summer and fall of 1861 near Camp Tompkins in Kanawha County. Here the various Confederate units from western Virginia were being recruited by Albert Jenkins and others. He was with his mother in the winter of 1862 and 1863 while they were living in Salem, Va. After the death of General Jenkins in 1864, James B. Bowlin, Virginia's father, was named guardian of James B. Jenkins and the other Jenkins children. The last mention of James B. in Cabell County records was in 1882. He was mentioned as one of the heirs at law of A. G. Jenkins, and stated that he was due a share in some property in Cincinnati, amounting to $4,992.04. It is believed that he probably went west to the St. Louis area about that time. James Bowlin Jenkins died on Feb. 4, 1888.

Alberta Gallatin Jenkins:

Alberta, the second child of Albert and Virginia, was born at Greenbottom on April 5, 1861. In Cabell County records of 1882, she is mentioned along with her guardian D. I. Smith as being one of the heirs of A. G. Jenkins, deceased. This settlement mentioned that she was due $4,842.24 from a share in some Cincinnati property. Alberta was also legally adopted by her grandfather, James B. Bowlin. Alberta lived with James B. Bowlin in St. Louis where she made her stage debut at the age of 25. Under the stage name of "Alberta Gallatin" she delighted the public in many Shakespearean roles, playing opposite many of the great actors of the day. She retired from the stage in 1920 at the age of 60. Twice she broke her retirement to return to the stage, the last time in 1940 as an old lady of 80. At that advanced age she revived the famous role of Mrs. Alving, in Ibsen's "Ghosts." In the 1930s Alberta lived at 128 West 77th Street in New York City and was married to Edwin Ogden Chiles. Alberta was the founder of the Edgar Allan Poe Society of America, with headquarters in New York City. She was still serving as "founder and president" in 1938. Her husband, Edwin, also served in several positions in the Poe Society in the 1930s. Alberta was invited but could not attend the dedication of the Jenkins Training School at Marshall University named in honor of her father in 1938. She died in New York City in 1948.

Margaret Virginia Jenkins:

The third child of Albert and Virginia was born April 25, 1863, at Salem, Va. She was born when the Jenkins family was rooming at Salem, while General Jenkins and his brigade were in winter quarters. Margaret Virginia never married. After her father's death, James B. Bowlin was named as her guardian. She was also mentioned in Cabell County records up to 1931. An estate settlement of 1882 mentioned that "Maggie" was one of the heirs of A. G. Jenkins, deceased. It stated she was due $4,992.04 for her share of property in Cincinnati. After the war Margaret Virginia went with her grandfather, James B. Bowlin, to St. Louis. She was educated in a Catholic convent in Ohio and in a Methodist academy in Kentucky. Supposedly, when she had grown, she returned each summer to the Greenbottom homestead. She then spent several years in Europe and traveled extensively across America, lecturing and pursuing educational work. She became an authority on Egyptian art and architecture. Around the turn of the century, Margaret spent almost 30 years in New York City, where she was engaged in library and school work. She lived within one block of Broadway. One wonders if she ever watched her sister perform in any of her wonderful stage plays. In the 1920s she was back living in the mansion at Greenbottom. There she planned and negotiated to turn her father's house over to the Huntington chapter of the United Daughters of the Confederacy. The mansion was to be restored to its original beauty and to be maintained as a memorial. By 1929 the estate had been reduced to only 155 acres, and the mansion was never turned over to the UDC. The Huntington "Herald-Advertiser" of Aug. 25, 1929, compared Margaret and her spirit to her father:

> "The daughter of this man who lives in the old homestead alone with her dreams and traditions is the incarnation of all that made her father famous. His unconquerable spirit is ablaze in her today as it was in him in '61. The culture and leadership that set him apart a man among men, is manifest in her. The stranger immediately feels he is in the presence, not of a person, but a personage."

Margaret Virginia was termed an "eccentric." It was related that in order to use the road that ran through the Jenkins property, people were made to pay "penalties" in the form of work. Since she lived alone, Margaret needed many chores performed around the old mansion. Therefore her "penalties" were mainly mowing brush, plowing, etc. The many people who talked to her stated that she would not mention her mother, but talked freely of her father.

In 1931 the last portion of the Jenkins estate passed to outsiders. Lola and Elliott Northcott took possession of the last of the estate, after over 100 years of ownership by the Jenkins family. For the next nine years Margaret Virginia lived in a house she called the Walnut Tree Lodge at Lesage, just south of Greenbottom. The United Daughters of the Confederacy did much to care for her in these last years. In the middle 1930s Margaret Virginia, even though very poor by that time, did provide funds for new windows in the Upper Greenbottom School.

In 1937 and 1938, Margaret Virginia furnished much information and photos of her father to the Works Progress Administration. The WPA had a large oil painting of Albert G. Jenkins painted, showing him in his general's uniform. This painting hung for years in the Jenkins Training School building on the campus of Marshall University. When the training school was dedicated on April 6, 1938, Margaret Virginia did attend, and sat in the crowd, not on the stage with her two cousins. She supposedly slipped out of the ceremony before it was finished.

In March of 1940, Margaret Virginia had the graves of her father and mother moved from the family cemetery at Greenbottom to a family plot she had purchased in Spring Hill Cemetery in Huntington. Also moved from Greenbottom were the graves of Eustatia Jenkins Lacy and C. B. McNutt Jenkins. Margaret Virginia died the next month, on April 9, 1940, in a Huntington hospital of heart disease. She was laid to rest in Spring Hill in the family plot with her parents and the two other members of her family she had worked so hard to move to their final resting place.

GEORGE JENKINS:

This child is mentioned here only because his name does appear in some traditional accounts of the Jenkins family. He was probably born in either 1862 or 1864, when his mother was traveling through Virginia during the war. George is not mentioned in the petition filed by James B. Bowlin before the Cabell County Board of Supervisors on June 4, 1867. This paper named the ". . . infant heirs of Albert G. Jenkins, deceased." Since it did name Virginia S. Jenkins as the widow and the other three children of Albert Jenkins, it is possible that George died before that date. George's name does not appear in any Cabell County records. Roy Bird Cook, famous West Virginia historian, mentioned in his notes that he did not find any evidence to support the fact that George was a child of Albert G. and Virginia Jenkins.

THE TERRITORIAL POLICY.

SPEECH OF ELI THAYER, OF MASS.,

IN REPLY TO

HON. MR. CURTIS AND HON. MR. GOOCH.

Delivered in the U. S. House of Representatives, May 11, 1860.

Mr. SPEAKER: I have listened with great interest to the remarks of my colleague, and also to those of the gentleman from Iowa, [Mr. CURTIS.] They have manifested suitable ingenuity in the discussion of this question; for, sir, it is the work of giants to prove to the people of this country that they have not a right to govern themselves, and that Congress has a right to govern them. That is a work that can be done only by giants. It is easy for ordinary men, for common men, to show to the people of this country that they have the right to govern themselves, and that they are abundantly prepared to exercise that right. In the early history of this Government, we had the Providence Plantations, the Plymouth colony, and the New Haven colony, which drummed out a Governor forced upon them by a non resident Power, and thereby secured to that State an indestructible possession—the proud history of the charter oak. Those men from the old country formed upon our soil model governments, and they did it without ever having had the experience afforded by the exercise of self-government.

But, sir, it is contended that we, who have always governed ourselves, when we go to a Territory of the United States are unable to tell our hands from our feet. It is contended that a man not only loses his rights, but loses his common sense, by going to a Territory. The gentleman from Iowa——

Mr. CURTIS. Mr. Speaker——

Mr. THAYER. I will allow no interruption. The gentleman from Iowa refused to let me ask him a question. I remember that.

Mr. CURTIS. I certainly did not, or at least I did not intend it.

Mr. THAYER. I shall not be interrupted. I have the floor.

Mr. CURTIS. I did not hear the gentleman, if he asked me any question.

Mr. THAYER. I was not astonished at the surprise which my colleague manifested, that I had taken the lead in this business of killing off these Territorial organizations which go upon the assumption that the people of a Territory are infants. Therefore I could understand the grief which he and the gentleman from Iowa must have felt when they saw that this leading and this voting was successful in the accomplishment of that result. Rachel mourned for her first-born, and would not be comforted. This day's slaughter of the innocents is no doubt an appropriate cause and occasion of grief.

Sir, grief may have a salutary influence upon men. The efforts of ingenuity and of invention may quicken their intellects. I am glad to see gentlemen striving for arguments that do not exist, and can never be found, showing why Congress should make an organic law for the people of the Territories, who are a thousand times better able than Congress to understand their wishes and necessities. There was need, sir, in this work, of quick and ready invention, of nervous struggling for expedients. We have witnessed all that this day—

"All the soul in rapt suspension;
All the quivering, palpitating
Chords of life in utmost tension
With the fervor of invention,
With the rapture of creating."

I said, grief itself may be salutary; and when these gentlemen see that they are in the minority, and that we who oppose their favorite measures are a majority in this House, I sympathize with them. I know something about the effect of defeat; and I say it, for their consolation, that I think it may be good. Sir, I have known something of the feeling of men who have experienced defeat; this feeling of distrust of the power of Providence to carry forward a good cause, this loss of faith in men, this ruinous and apparently crushing despair, *may* sometimes work great good. The pearl is only the crystallized tear of the oyster.

Mr. GOOCH rose.

Mr. THAYER. I will not be interrupted.

Mr. GOOCH. I say to my colleague, that I allowed him to interrupt me frequently during my remarks on the polygamy bill, a few days ago; and yet he is not willing to give me the same privilege.

Mr. THAYER. If my colleague wishes to interrupt me, I will allow him to do anything he chooses. [Laughter.]

Mr. GOOCH. I thought my colleague would not be as unjust as he intimated. I must express some surprise at the reference my colleague has made. If he had looked up his quotations to express surprise, instead of grief, it would have been more to the purpose. I expressed no grief. I simply expressed surprise.

Eli Thayer was a strong opponent of Jenkins over the colonization of Ceredo, a town just to the west of Huntington.

NOTES TO "HISTORY OF AGRICULTURE"

The following pages are a transcription of an original paper in the Special Collections of the James E. Morrow Library at Marshall University in Huntington, W.Va. The paper has been attributed to Albert Gallatin Jenkins, but it is incomplete and unsigned. The paper had belonged to the West Virginia historian, Roy Bird Cook, in 1916. Cook sent the manuscript to Fred B. Lambert, then a teacher at Barboursville in Cabell County. It then passed with the Lambert papers into the Special Collection at Marshall. It is obviously a rough draft, with many corrections and some marginal notes. A handwriting analysis was conducted, comparing several words in this paper with three original letters signed by Jenkins. The similarities are exact and distinct. Jenkins was very distinctive in his formation of certain words, especially "the" and "of." It was obvious to all of us who examined the documents that this paper was indeed written by Albert Gallatin Jenkins.

Our next problem was to date the paper. Three things were determining factors in that dating: 1. The actual paper which Jenkins used for the essay. Each of the eight pages was stamped with the mark: "Taylor & Maury, Washington." The paper was of heavy quality, probably a fine linen. An original letter, signed by Jenkins and dated 1860, exists at West Virginia University. The paper used in that letter bears the same embossed mark as the paper on agriculture. 2. The wording of the paper. Jenkins used many Greek, Roman, and Egyptian sources, and obviously had access to or knew a great deal about these cultures and the philosophers. The language is fairly polished and demonstrated his excellent vocabulary. This is consistent with what we know of Jenkins' education. 3. His reference to the "... History of Greece by Mr. Grote published some twelve or fifteen years ago. ..." Mr. Grote's twelve volumes on Greece were first published in 1846. From these three factors, we conclude that the paper was written between the years 1858 and 1861, probably when Jenkins was a U. S. Congressman, living in Washington. It was probably written at the request of some of his constituency, and was intended to be notes for a speech on agriculture.

"History of Agriculture"
by
Albert Gallatin Jenkins

In attempting to take a brief and concise view of the History of Agriculture for practical purposes it is obviously necessary for us to pass by the speculative questions connected with the origin of the Human race, the fall of our fore-parents and the curse which thereafter prevented the spontaneous production of the Earth as in the Bible and so fully and variously treated of by commentators. We will also find it necessary for many reasons to omit any examination into the subject for many ages after the period alluded to. The only means of information being occasional allusions by the authors of the old Testament familiar to all allusions so unfrequent and remote as to leave us almost to vague conjecture at last. It will be sufficient for these reasons therefore for us to begin the examination of our subject at a period not so distant but that our pathway may be lighted up by the Historical records of Grecian & Roman civilizations. And even then the paucity of materials in the way of historical evidences upon the subject is frequently so great as to make it necessary as almost to dispose of centuries in a sentence. War and its vicisitudes form almost exclusively the subject matter of history; and he who enters upon an historical examination of a subject not mainly connected therewith will at once be struck with the scantiness of information to be adduced. This may lead us to condemn the Historian; but we must be more sparing of our censure when we remember that much of the blame should attach to the readers of History; for so long as the public mind delights to revel in the spectacle of "all the glorious pomp & circumstance of war" so long will writers

In attempting to take a brief and concise view of the History of Agriculture for practical purposes it is obviously necessary for us to pass by the speculative questions connected with ~~the creation of the world and~~ the origin of the Human race — the fall of our fore-parents and the curse which thereafter prevented the spontaneous productions of the Earth, as in the Bible and so fully and variously treated of by Commentators. We will also find it necessary for many reasons to omit any examination into the subject in the earlier ages for many ages after the period alluded to. The only means of information being occasional allusions by the authors of the Old Testament familiar to all, allusions so unfrequent and remote as to leave us almost to vague conjecture at last. It will be sufficient for these reasons therefore for us to begin the examination of our subject at a period not so distant but that our pathway may be lighted up by the Historical records of Grecian & Roman Civilization.

First page of the draft "History of Agriculture." It was written by Albert G. Jenkins probably between 1858 and 1861. The watermark in the upper left corner of the paper reads: "Taylor & Maury, Washington." Courtesy: Morrow Library, Marshall University covetous of public applause exhibit them prominent in the foreground of historical sketches. It may seem a strange fact too that this characteristic is, if possible more applicable to modern than ancient Historians. As an evidence of this I will call your attention to one among a number of instance leading to that conclusion. In the History of Greece by Mr. Grote published some twelve or fifteen years ago comprising twelve volumes and which has gained a world wide celebrity for the author, there is not a single remark *bestowed* upon the agricultural pursuits of the people whose history he recounts. And indeed it is chiefly in the original histories of the Ancients themselves—in the lives of their great men—and in the incidents that are recorded of them that we are enabled to glean what may be known of the Agriculture of former ages.

In taking a survey then of the History Agriculture under the limits & restrictions we have just placed upon ourselves it will perhaps be most in the order of chronology first to turn our attention to Egypt, famed as she has been for ages for the fruitfulness of her soil and the remarkable means which so much contribute to that result. Considering Ancient Egypt as including what has sometimes been called upper - Middle & Lower Egypt we have but a comparatively small extent of territory—traversed by the river Nile through its whole length whose "bottoms" as we would say vary from fifteen to one hundred & fifty miles in breadth. And yet we are told by Heroditus that in the time of Amasis Egypt could boast of twenty thousand cities well inhabited. And Diodonus Sicilus relates that in a general account once taken there were seven million of peoples. This will serve at once to give us some idea of the state of agriculture which could support such an immense population on a comparatively small extent of territory(?). In addition to this we must remember that Egypt was at this time a corn *exporting* country. We must still farther remember that corn by which of course is meant wheat barley & c and not the Indian Maize to designate which we use the term in America, was not the only purpose to which the cultivation of the soil was applied. Among other things we may mention papyrus—from which paper for various purposes was manufactured. Abestinum which Pliny describes as an incombustible flax—Linum also a species of flax—Byssus still another rarity of flax from which a very fine & delicate linen was made. Lotus a plant from whose berries head was made in a very early age. Besides fruits melons and vegetables of almost infinite variety. The inundations of the Nile were of course the immediate cause of the prosperity of agriculture in Ancient Egypt. But nature thus left to herself would have accomplished but little for the irrigation & enriching of the soil as but a small extent of land would have been inundated and that only temporarily; but with the aid of vast reservoirs, canals & sluices constructed for the purpose the mighty flood of the Nile was gathered and controlled for future uses of irrigation as the wants of the husbandman might require. We must not here omit to notice the lake Moeris which if constructed by human ingenuity is the most stupendous relic of the achievements of mankind, and which if fashioned by nature and applied by the ingenuity of man to the purposes of irrigating the soil is still wonderful to consider. Herodotus & contemporay historians describe this lake to have been constructed by King Moeris from whom it takes its name and to have been excavated for the purpose of receiving and holding the waters of the Nile when rising to a great height and to be distributed therefrom afterwards for irrigating purposes. They describe it to have been three thousand and six hundred stadia (or about four hundred & fifty of our English miles in circumference). They agree in representing it as being two hundred cubits deep (about three hundred English feet.) Tomponius Mela gives a still larger estimate of its dimensions. Modern travellers however, among whom may be mentioned Larcher Pococke Norden & Sarvery all represent the present size of this lake or reservoir as being less than we have described—most of them estimating it at fifty leagues in circumference. But when taken at this estimate it would require the Ohio river if emptying into it at an ordinary(?) stage of water say half a mile wide & surveying five feet deep & running at a rate of four miles per hour over six years to fill it. Scarcely less remarkable is the canal by which the waters of the Nile were drawn off into the lake. This still remains entire—it is called the Bahn Youseff or river Joseph. What splendid evidences have we here of the magnitude of the agricultural interests of this wonderful land. The devotion of prince & people to the successful cultivation of the soil is attested by all historians. For almost countless ages Egypt was the grainary of the civilized world—and what she did in the time of Joseph, rescuing neighboring nations from the horrors of famine she continued to do for centuries thereafter.

Political changes—with absolute conquest its attendent horrors seemed impotent in a contest with the acricultural prosperity of this remarkable country. And as the prince of the various countries whose arms rendered her tributary she still proudly boasted that though conquered she fed her conquerors.

We have spoken of the great esteem in which agricultural pursuits are held in ancient Egypt. So far did this extend that the very profession of husbandmen was of itself a title to respectability to have abject a condition the party professing it might be reduced. The same sentiment in a modified degree extended to shepherds, But there was a remarkable exception in the case of swineherds—the latter from the supposed impunity of the animal being held in great detestation throughout all Egypt. No one would give them his daughter in marriage and they were not even permitted to enter the temples. We have said that this prejudice against swineherds originated in the disgust which the Egyptians entertained for swine. So great was the latter that if an Egyptian casually touched a hog he immediately plunged clothes & all into the water.

A brief allusion to the productiveness of the soil of Egypt under this system of agriculture as compared with our own and we shall turn our attention to another question. It is confidently stated by various ancient authorities that such was the fertility of the soil of Egypt that a grain of wheat would produce one hundred & fifty eavs(?) —or heads as we would term them. But this evidently did not mean as cultivated for a crop—It was plainly intended to refer to a grain of wheat isolated from others and cultivated for the especial purpose of generating as many shoots as possible; for we have the best authority for knowing that in the production of a crop of wheat a yield of ten fold was considered a good one. And though it is impossible to ascertain the exact standard between ancient & modern weights & measures they can be very nearly approximated, and upon this approximation we ascertain the quantity of wheat usually sown to the acre in Egypt to have been about one hundred & twenty pounds or two bushels English measure—And at the ratio of a tenfold increase the production would be twenty bushels English measure per acre.

But with the cursory glance our subject which our limits require we have already dwealt longer than we should have done upon Egyptian agriculture. Let us now turn our attention to the next and indeed a cotemporeanous theatre of human civilization-we mean that part of Asia known as India & Persia, also what is called the Assyrian Empire. Little or nothing is known of the arts & sciences of earlier ages of this portion of the Human race now of the brief allusion in sacred history, except what we derive from the pages of Zenephon & Heroditus to whom tradition furnished what little they have recorded. We know nothing of the method of agriculture—nothing of the esteem or disesteem in which it was held—nothing of the extent to which it was carried save what we may infer from the density of population which it sustained; until the reign of Cyrus who reduced this vast & diversified region to a single empire. This prince so renowned in war was the ——?—— patron of agriculture. Every means were resorted to by this wise monarch for the encouragement of agricultural pursuits among his people. Presents or prizes instituted by him to the most successful; and laying off fields groves & gardens and often planting with his own hands in order that by imitation of royal example his people might be led to apply themselves to this branch of industry. The Satraps too were held to a scrupulous account for the manner in which agriculture was carried on in their respective provinces. Indeed under the reign of Cyrus the whole agricultural art seems to have systematized and to have flourished with a degree of prosperity hitherto unknown. This too was its zenith—for under the cruel & disastrous rule of his son & successor Cambyses agriculture shared in the common decline which attended all the useful arts & sciences and under the inglorious reigns of subsequent soverigns the luxurious arts & the perilous and effeminate tastes and pursuits which prevailed in Persia proper extended trenches over the whole empire. Agriculture claimed to be respected as an ennobling occupation; and the plunder which conquest achieved in earlier times still enabled them to lay upon other nations supplied the grainaries which their own industry left unfilled. Such was the condition of matters at the time of their early intercourse with the Greeks. And of the latter it is now necessary to speak.

In turning our attention then to agriculture among the Ancient Greeks we must set out by confessing our regret that this useful & ennobling employment was held in so little esteem by this gifted people. There were indeed a few emminent persons at different periods of her history numbering some of her most distinguished philosophers of whom we may particularly mention Socrates who sought but without success to instill different sentiments into the minds of the people. Some of these translated into the Grecian tongue all the most celebrated agricultural writings but agriculture still remained as before—holding a subordinate place in the esteem of the Greeks. We may judge of the ill success of Socrates in his undertaking when we remember that both Plato & Aristotle who of all others we would suppose most likely to be influenced by his precepts, both speak of agriculture as indeed necessary for the prosperity of the state, but as being utterly unfit for freeborn citizens and ought only to be countenanced in slaves.

It would be interesting to ascertain if possible the substantial causes for the slight esteem in which agriculture was held & the limited manner in which it was practiced by this free & enlightened people. These reasons we think are as follows—1st the soil of a portion of Greece especially Attica was rugged in character and for the most part sterile & nonproductive except of the olive & the Grape—2nd the peculiar system of laws which early lawyers stamped almost ineffaceably upon the policy of the various kingdoms were from the very nature destructive of agriculture pursuits on the part of the free citizens. This remark is particularly applicable to Sparta—3rd & lastly the Mecural temper of the people, which rendered the unexciting occupation of agriculture distasteful and could only be satisfied with a career of arms or in the animating rivalry of the fine arts.

I had intended to close this brief notice agriculture in Greece with the translations of a few extracts from Zenophan detailing a conversation between Socrates & a practical farmer called Isomachus; but I must content myself by simply referring to it and recommending it for perusal to my young farmer friends if they decide to be both interested & instructed. It is here that is noted the celebrated answer of the Persian King who being asked what made his horse so fast replied *The Eye of his Master*. It is on this occasion too that Isomachus advises one in choosing a steward for his farm never to select either of the following classes—1st a man who sleeps late—2nd a man who drinks much & 3rd a man who is in love. For these three classes he says can't properly attend to their own affairs, much less other peoples. And he particularly cautions his friends in looking for a manager of their estates to give the latter—the man in love—a wide berth, evidently regarding him as being only one degree removed from a crazy man, an opinion however which I have no doubt some young gentlemen now present would most indignantly repudiate.

In this same conversation between Socrates and Isomachus upon husbandry are to be found some excellent sayings upon household economy which might be valuable to the female portion of my audience unless indeed their sympathy with Xantippe in the family quarrels of the philosophers should prejudice in them against receiving instruction from such a source.

Perhaps it would be proper before closing our notice of Grecian agriculture to give a few facts in detail connected therewith. Agricultural implements were partially made of iron—and were various in character, even the plow was constructed upon several different plans. Wheat was always sown broadcast by the hand as is common with us now. It was always sown if possible after the first rain in September, seeming to regard that as a sort of invitation extended by the Gods to the Husbandman to sow, and a promise on their part that they would be propitious. It was considered best by way of preparing the soil for sowing wheat to plough it in the spring and stir it again in the summer. When ripe the grain was reaped with a scythe and the stubble remaining upon the ground usually burnt. The grain was threshed from the straw just as we have all seen it done here a few years ago only laying the sheaves in the form of a circle and then driving or riding horses or oxen around upon it and thus tramping out the grain with the hoof.

The olive was principally cultivated in Attica—but the grape throughout all Greece; these wines of which were famous throughout the limits of civilization. In this respect Italy—afterwards so renouned for her wines was centuries behind. These wines held in greatest repute were those of Cyprus, Chio & Lesbos. They were sweet to the palate and mild & harmless in character, being very different in this respect from the wines in the Homeric age, if we may credit the account of the great poet himself who speaks of a wine which it was necessary to mix with twenty times its own quantity of water in order to bring it down to a proper degree of strength. Unless we are willing to credit this somewhat remarkable statement we can only conclude that the poet having bestowed such incredible strength upon his heroes felt bound by poetical consistency to do no less by his wines.

And now let us take leave of Grecian agriculture and following the course of history turn our attention to a chapter upon which the enlightened agriculturist of the present age—especially if he be a citizen of this Republican land of ours loves above all others to dwell—I mean the chapter which recounts the history of Roman Civilization. The Greeks—a few of their philosophers rather, speculated about agriculture as they did about everything else—but the Romans practiced it as a nation. It ranked in dignity of pursuit before all other occupations and indeed was esteemed the only honorable one for a Roman citizen. We speak now of the palmy days of Rome. When her consuls returning victorious from every clime and laying conquered empires at the feet of the Republic eagerly sought out their farms the old homesteads and then joyfully mingled in the everyday occupation of a farmers life directing their slaves and sharing their labors—guiding the plow with the hand in whose grasp the spear struck terror to the enemies of the Republic. In those happy times when, as Pliny remarks, the earth glorious in seeing herself cultivated by the hands of triumphant victors seemed to make new efforts and to produce her fruits in greater abundance. Dionyses Halicarnassus relates that even as far back as the time of Numa Tompilius agricultural pursuits were made the subject of governmental care. The whole Roman Territory was laid off into districts or cantons. Full details of the extent & manner of cultivation were required of each canton—and every pains taken to promote and encourage this branch of industry. Ancus Martius followed the same line of policy, and placed the cultivation of the soil second only to the worship of the gods as a duty of a free citizen. What was so worthily begun under the early kings of Rome continued during the existence of the Republic proper. Agriculture was so to speak a national institution, the comfort of the poor, the pride of the rich and the practice of all. Roman Senators habitually resided upon their estates and only came to the city as our country magistrates now come to town—on public days when their presence was requisite. He who tilled his farm badly received the condemnation of the censor and the sensure of the Republic. Varieties of grain which are now common in Europe & America were extensively cultivated in the territory belonging to Rome—(except of course Indian Maize or what we usually term corn) Fruits were also grown to great perfection. The apple was indiginous to Italy, and the orange—the apricot—the peach, the citron & the pomegranate were all introduced from foreign countries and successfully cultivated. The olive was also introduced about two centuries after the foundation of Rome. The prejudices of the ancients that it required a very hot climate and besides could be grown near the seashore were overcome by experience and the culture of the olive extended almost throughout Italy. The cultivation of flax was introduced from Egypt and proved a great source of wealth to the Roman provinces. What we called artificial grass, of different varieties were also tried and being successful came into general use. The herding of cattle was also extensively engaged in and supposed to be the source of much profit. But the culture of the grape was not behind any other employment of the agriculturalist either in the extent to which it was carried or the reputation it enjoyed. Thus agriculture flourished for centuries throughout the Roman Commonwealth. We have before remarked that it seemed to be a national institution with the Romans; and its history would seem to justify the observation, for unlike many other arts in many other countries and unlike some even in Rome which seemed to prosper upon the decline of the commonwealth and to grow fat by feeding upon the decaying vitals of the Republic—agriculture on the contrary grew with its growth strengthened with its strength and declined with its decay. There were indeed some immediate causes the operation of which bettered agricultural pursuits, but he who seeks for the real causes must look for them in those which induced the decline of the Republic itself.

In the time of Cato, or about two centuries before the Christian era, agriculture may be said to have reached its zenith and even to have commenced its decline. Cato himself was a Roman of the old school who when not serving his country in some public capacity was quietly cultivating his farm. He himself was a writer upon agriculture—his "De Re Rustica" entering fully and minutely into all the details of practical farming. Cato had a neighbor Manius Cervius Dentatus whose farm adjoined his own and whose example he tells us did much in teaching him the true economy of farming. This old Roman neighbor was at the time one of the most emminent men in the commonwealth. Thrice had he been honored with a triumph. And yet he now lived upon an humble estate, using the greatest simplicity of dress and frugality of diet. Here remarks Cato he was approached by the ambassadors of the Samnites who found him dining upon the coarsest fare, and in attempting to bribe him with an immense sum of money received this reply—"Gold is of but little value to a man who can be satisfied with such a dinner, and I think it more glorious to conquer those that have that gold than to posses it myself." It was from such a character that Cato drew the mold of his own. It is related of the latter that with all his reputation for economy he was nevertheless reproached on a certain occasion by one of his friends for his extravagence who had heard that Cato gave the same wine to his servants to drink that he drank himself; but Cato replied that his servants did not drink the same wine that he did, but he drank the same wine that they did. Here in a seeming solecism we cannot fail to detect a bit of household economy most fittingly expressed. Cato in describing the Solitaunilia—a ceremony in which the husbandmen were wont to propitiate the farms towards the forthcoming crops recites the following prayer, which was uttered while libations were being poured on the altars, and as it may be interesting to know how our brother farmers prayed two thousand years ago we will give a translation of it. "Father May I humbly implore & conjure you to be propitious and favorable to me my family and all my domestics in regard to the occasion of the present procession in my fields, land & estate, to prevent—avert and remove from us all diseases known & unknown—desolations storms calamaties and pestilential air; to make our plants, corn, vines & trees grow and come to perfection; to preserve our shepherds and flocks; to grant thy preservation of life & health to me my family & all my domestics."

From the time of Cato agriculture rapidly continued to decline which it had already begun, both as regards the extent to which it was carried & the esteem in which it was held though it still continued to be the pregnant theme of poetry and often the subject of practical treatises. Among the latter we may mention the agricultural writings of Barro who lived more than a century after Cato. After another century comes Columella who writes copiously upon the subject of agriculture and pathetically laments the decline into which such an honorable pursuit had fallen. "I see at Rome said he, the schools of philosophers—rhetoricians geometricians, and what is more astonishing of people solely employed, some in preparing dishes proper to whet the apetite and excite gluttony, and others to adorn the head with artificial curls, but not one for agriculture."

Indeed at the time when this author wrote Rome had already become dependent upon foreign countries for bread. Sicily—Sardinia—Carthage & Egypt were principally relied upon. The Mistress of the world, her citizens corrupted by the accumulated wealth of the plunder of centuries, and public and private virtue sapped by the vices it engendered, agriculture at length ceased to be thought of as a fitting occupation for Roman citizens. The people received largess of corn olive oil & wine or money either from those in power or those aspiring to be so; and he who was most lavish in disturbing public property was regarded as the proper person to guide the helm of state. Thus Roman agriculture—once the pride and glory of the nation, became practically extinct. The feeble existence it afterwards maintained until the final eruption of the barbarians who overthrew the Roman empire is hardly deserving of a passing notice. Nor is it compatible with the limits of this dissertation for us to trace the decline of agriculture in the remote provinces of the Roman government. This like the other arts & sciences which had lighted up the face of the globe was at length enveloped in the gloom of the "*Dark ages*—into whose murky depths the eye of the historian" may pay in vain in attempting to discover anything radiant with civilization. Poetry—painting—music—sculpture—oratory—history—architecture—commerce and agriculture are alike extinguished in a common night. War, desolating war nagging incessantly; carried on in every scale from the banding together of vast nations in a common cause animated by a fanaticism as remarkable for its fury as for its absurdity, down to the depredations of a petty lord upon the rights of his neighbor. So great were the effects of this state of things upon agriculture that from the fifth to the eleventh century land was comparatively valueless. Immense tracts of country were sold for the smallest consideration, and frequently given away in lavish profusion to favorites, or bequeathed to the church of Rome. But from this universal night—from this chaos of gloom & confusion order & light, at length made their appearance. Early in the catalogue of the arts and sciences which reappeared we find the occupation of agriculture. And it may be asked to whom are we to award the credit of this. History universally awards it to the monks of the Catholic church. The monasteries possessing immense grants of lands, the funds necessary for their improvement, and the priests of the order leading a quiet and secluded life, agriculture seemed to be an occupation to which they naturally inclined. To them too we are indebted for the preservation of the writings of ancient authors upon the subject of agriculture, and the perpetuation of the race of many useful plants vegetables & cereals. The influence of their example soon extended to the adjoining laity who were gradually persuaded to give up the chase as well as their predatory excursions against their neighbors and to find a less precarious livelyhood in the cultivation of the soil; thus establishing a solid basis upon which the structure of civilization with all its adornments of the arts & sciences was subsequently reared, in the various countries which comprised modern Europe. We have said that the credit of the restoration of agriculture from the wretched condition into which it finally fell during the period of the Dark ages was due to the Roman Catholic clergy. There is one remarkable exception to this obtrusive universal truth—and that is to be found in the case of Spain. An exception so peculiar & extraordinary that we would do injustice to our subject even in so brief an historical sketch if we were to pass it by in silence. In a word their agriculture in Spain owes its preservation its progression and some of its greatest achievements to the invasion of the Saracens about the beginning of the 8th century. These more liberal than many han—?— of the Teutonic race who overran the other western provinces of the Roman empire permitted the former population to remain in peace & security and indeed to be protected by their arms upon the sole condition of yielding allegience to the invaders. Nay the very possessors of the soil were upon the same conditions permitted in most cases full & undisturbed enjoyment of all the ancient privileges. And though the ancient nobility for the most part refused to accept a boon so galling to their pride the middle & lower classes were less sensitive in that regard. Indeed the Spanish peasantry were in all substantial respects gainers instead of losers by the Saracenic invasion. And notwithstanding their migratory character we must remember that the Arabs who overran Spain must be considered as an agricultural people. They initiated & perfected the system of irrigation in the southern portion of Spain which even at this time pervails. Sugar which is now hardly at all raised in Spain proper was so successfully cultivated by the Saracens that it not only supplied home consumption but was largely exported. Vegetables were grown with a care & success never since approached—many varieties of esculents then in vogue and no longer to be found in use. Their writers too upon agricultural subjects were numerous. Indeed the evidences are numerous on every side tending to show that to the Saracenic invasion Spain is indebted for the prosperous state of agriculture prevailing up to the time of their final expulsion. Such was its condition when the Spaniards proper recovered possession of the country and Christian sovereigns—so called—succeeded to the Spanish throne. Under these agriculture for some time continued the impetus it received from the Saracens, until the discovery of America—and the subjection of a vast portion of it to their dominion with their almost fabulous mines of gold and silver discouraged the tame pursuit of agriculture in the mother land. The unhappy effects which this state of things inflicted upon the agricultural interests of Spain was rendered still more disastrous by the wretched government to which Spain was soon after subjected and which have continued almost uninterruptedly from that period to the present time terminating finally in the miserable agriculture—the supressed commerce—the hampered & restricted manufacturies which the eye of modern traveler now beholds throughout the length & breadth of Spain.

But my limits warn me not to indulge in even so brief a review of the history of agriculture in the various provinces of the Roman Empire which now compose the kingdoms of Europe. Having rapidly sketched that of Spain forming such a peculiar exception to the general history of these kingdoms and the other being strikingly like each other in the general features of the history of the rise & progress of agriculture, I will briefly notice but a single one. In making this selection the instincts of a common race would lead us almost involuntarily to turn to England—a proud old ancestress against whose tyranny we rebelled, but around whose name and whose fame in spite of us will cluster the fillial sympathies of their descendants whom every page of modern history as it recounts the conceptions of their genius—the achievements of their energy and the trophies of their valor proclaims to be the lineal offspring of the parent stock.

We have before spoken of agriculture as being viewed throughout Europe (except in the case of Spain) from the state of decay into which it had fallen in the dark ages, by the monks of the various monasteries to which large donations of land had been made. As far down as the 11th century the condition of agriculture in England was piteous in the extreme. From the Domesday book may be gathered the most abundant evidence of this fact. The occupied lands of a whole manor which would now be a fortune for an English gentleman are sometimes returned in the Domesday book at a value as low as forty shillings. Making every allowance for the difference in the value of money at that age & the present and the wretchedness of the state of agriculture still seems to be incredible. The returns of the Domesday book also show conclusively that the cultivation of the church lands was in advance of the rest. Ingulfus(?) Abbot of Croyland speaks of an early attempt to impair the condition of agriculture by Richard de Rules Lord of Deeping who "obtained permission of the abbey to enclose a large portion of marsh for the purpose of seperate pasture" and which he brought to be as fertile as a garden. This example soon extended its influence and the inhabitants of the town of Spalding divided their marshes out among them some draining & tilling them—others counting(?) them into pastures & c. This soon led to the same action on the part of other villages. Thus agriculture made some little progress. In the thirteenth century a considerable degree had been attained. Yet even at this period the rent of land—and the best land—was only a shilling per acre, when cultivated in grain or vegetables. But it is curious to remark that *meadow land* rented for two or three shillings per acre.

At this time neither wheat nor barley were allowed to be exported. It may be interesting to notice the price of agricultural products at this time. Wheat sold for about the tenth of the sum it now commands. Barley at about the same relative price. The price of cattle & c were equally low—an ox sold for ten or twelve shillings say two dollars or two & a half of our currency. The price of a sheep was a single shilling. It will at once occur to us to inquire how it could be that grain, cattle & c when the soil was so badly tilled & cattle so little reared should still be ten times cheaper than they are now? The answer is easy and is to be found in the difference of the value of money at that time & the present. Thus though grain and cattle were only one tenth of their present value in money, yet at that time money itself was about twenty five times more valueable than it is now. It is also curious to observe as affecting the state of agriculture that a minimum price was fixed by law below which certain products should not be sold. Thus wheat could not be sold below 4S. 8 pence per quarter. The wages paid to farm hands were also regulated by law. In 1350 harvest laborers were allowed wages not to exceed 3 1/2 pence per day without board—a little more than a century afterwards they were fixed at five pence without board. Another half century later and a law was passed allowing no farm hand to be paid more than 18 shillings a year & board—or say 4 dollars & a half in our currency. In the meantime however agriculture was improving. Finally a more enlightened spirit repealed many of the legislative restrictions upon husbandry. Many new vegetables were introduced into England from foreign countries. Most of these however not farther back than the Reign of Elizabeth & Mary of them(?) subsequently(?). From that period to the present century the improvement in agri

(incomplete, last page or pages missing)

Bibliography

BOOKS AND PAMPHLETS

Ambler, Charles Henry. *West Virginia Stories and Biographies.* New York: Rand McNally & Co., 1942.

Bradford, Gamaliel. *Confederate Portraits.* New York: Houghton-Mifflin Co., 1914.

Cohen, Stan. *The Civil War in West Virginia.* Charleston: Pictorial Histories Pub. Co., 1979.

Comstock, Jim. *The West Virginia Heritage Encyclopedia.* Richwood, W.Va.: 1974.

Davis, William C. (editor). *The Image of War: 1861-1865, Vol. 1 Shadows of the Storm.* Garden City, N.Y.: Doubleday & Co., 1981.

Dawson, John Harper. *Wildcat Cavalry, A Synoptic History of the Seventeenth Virginia Cavalry Regiment.* Dayton: Morningside House, 1982.

Dickinson, Jack L. *Records of the 16th Regiment Virginia Cavalry, C.S.A.* Huntington, W.Va.: 1984.

__________. *8th Virginia Cavalry.* Lynchburg, VA: H. E. Howard, 1986.

Evans, Clement A. (general editor). *Confederate Military History* (13 volumes), Atlanta: Confederate Pub. Co., 1899. (West Virginia volume.)

Freeman, Douglas Southall. *Lee's Lieutenants.* New York: Charles Scribner's Sons, 1942. 3 volumes.

Givens, Lula Porterfield. *Highlights in the Early History of Montgomery County, Virginia.* Pulaski, Va.: B. D. Smith & Bros., 1975.

Hardee, William J. *Rifle and Light Infantry Tactics.* New York: J.O. Kane Publ., 1862.

Hardesty, H. H. *Hardesty's History of Putnam County.* New York: H. H. Hardesty & Co., 1883.

Johnson, Patricia Givens. *The United States Army Invades The New River Valley May 1864.* Christiansburg, Va.: Walpa Publishing, 1986.

Johnston, David E. *A History of Middle New River Settlements.* Radford, Va.: Commonwealth Press, 1969.

Longacre, Edward G. *The Cavalry at Gettysburg.* Cranbury, N.J.: Associated University Presses, 1986.

Lowry, Terry. *September Blood, The Battle of Carnifex Ferry.* Charleston: Pictorial Histories Pub. Co., 1985.

__________. *The Battle of Scary Creek.* Charleston: Pictorial Histories Pub. Co., 1982.

Randall, J. G. and Donald, David H. *The Civil War and Reconstruction.* Lexington, Mass.: D. C. Heath & Co., 1969.

Riggs, David F. *East of Gettysburg, Custer vs. Stuart.* Revised Edition. Ft. Collins, Colo.: The Old Army Press, 1985.

Smith, Wiatt (editor). *Guyandotte Centennial 1810-1910.* Published by: The Guyandotte Centennial and Cabell County Home Coming Association, 1910.

Stutler, Boyd. *The Civil War in West Virginia.* Charleston: Education Foundation, Inc., 1963.

United States War Department. *War of the Rebellion: A Compilation of the Official Records of the Union and Confederate Armies.* (128 volumes) Washington, D.C.: Government Printing Office, 1880-1901.

Wakelyn, Jon. L. *Biographic Dictionary of the Confederacy.* Westport, Conn.: Greenwood Press, 1977.

Wallace, George Seldon. *Cabell County Annals and Families.* Richmond: Garrett & Massie, 1935.

Wallace, Lee A., Jr. *A guide to Virginia Military Organizations 1861-1865.* Richmond: Virginia Civil War Commission, 1964.

Wintz, William D. (editor). *The History of Putnam County.* Charleston, W.Va.: Upper Vandalia Historical Society, 1983.

MAGAZINES AND JOURNALS

Levi Welch, "Battle of Scary," *West Virginia Historical Quarterly,* Vol. 1, No. 1, Jan. 1901.

Roy Bird Cook, "Albert Gallatin Jenkins—A Confederate Portrait," *West Virginia Review,* No. 11, May 1934.

MANUSCRIPTS AND CORRESPONDENCE

Correspondence from Edgar A. Poe Society, Baltimore, Md.

Correspondence from Harvard University Archives, Cambridge, Mass.

Correspondence from Margaret Virginia Jenkins, 1936-1937, Special Collections, Morrow Library, Marshall University.

Correspondence from Oberlin College, Oberlin, Ohio.

Correspondence from Virginia Military Institute, Lexington, Va.

Correspondence from Washington and Jefferson College, Washington, Pa.

"Diary of a Border Ranger," James D. Sedinger, Co. E, 8th Virginia Cavalry. Unpublished narrative at the West Virginia Archives, Charleston, W.Va.

DuFeu, E. L., "When Lee Marched Over the Mountain Wall," unpublished, 1984.

French, S. Bassett, Biographical sketches. The Virginia State Library, Richmond.

"Jenkins' Brigade in the Gettysburg Campaign," diary of Lt. Hermann Schuricht (14th Virginia Cavalry), Southern Historical Papers, Vol. XXIV, Richmond, 1896.

Johnson, Flora Smith, "The Civil War Record of Albert Gallatin Jenkins." A report submitted toward requirements for Master of Arts Degree, Marshall College, 1944.

Nelson, Hon. C. P., "Albert Gallatin Jenkins." A speech given at dedication of A. G. Jenkins Hall, Marshall University, Huntington, W.Va., 1937.

Remarks by Dr. Alexander McCausland at Carnifex Ferry Battlefield Park, Sept. 14, 1986.

Teays, Victoria Hansford, "Reminiscences of the War in West Virginia," personal collection of Bill Wintz.

Veterans Grave Registration of West Virginia. A WPA project. Card file located at the West Virginia Archives.

NEWSPAPERS AND NEWSPAPER ARTICLES

Huntington Advertiser, articles by Ken Hechler, 1961.

Kanawha Valley Star, Charleston, Va. July 27, 1858—April 9, 1861, Microfilm Collection, West Virginia Archives.

The Guerilla, Charleston, Va., Sept. 29, 1862.

The Ironton Register, Ironton, Ohio, 1861-1864.

The Parkersburg News, Parkersburg, W.Va., June 21 and Dec. 20, 1964.

The Southern Illustrated News, Richmond, Oct. 31, 1863.

COURTHOUSE RECORDS AND MISCELLANEOUS SOURCES

Burial records of Spring Hill Cemetery, Huntington, W.Va.

Genealogical records at the Latter Day Saints (Mormon) Church Genealogical Library, Huntington, W.Va.

Papers of Roy Bird Cook, West Virginia Collection, Colson Hall, West Virginia University, Morgantown, W.Va.

Vital records of Cabell County, W.Va. Courthouse, Huntington, W.Va.

Vital records of Hamilton County, Ohio. Courthouse, Cincinnati, Ohio.

Vital records of Lawrence County, Ohio. Courthouse, Ironton, Ohio.

Vital records of Rockbridge County, Va. Courthouse, Lexington, Va.

INDEX

The two principal topics of this book are not entered in this index: Albert Gallatin Jenkins and Greenbottom. Towns, counties, and other locations are assumed to be found within the state of Virginia, (or that part that later became West Virginia,) unless otherwise noted.

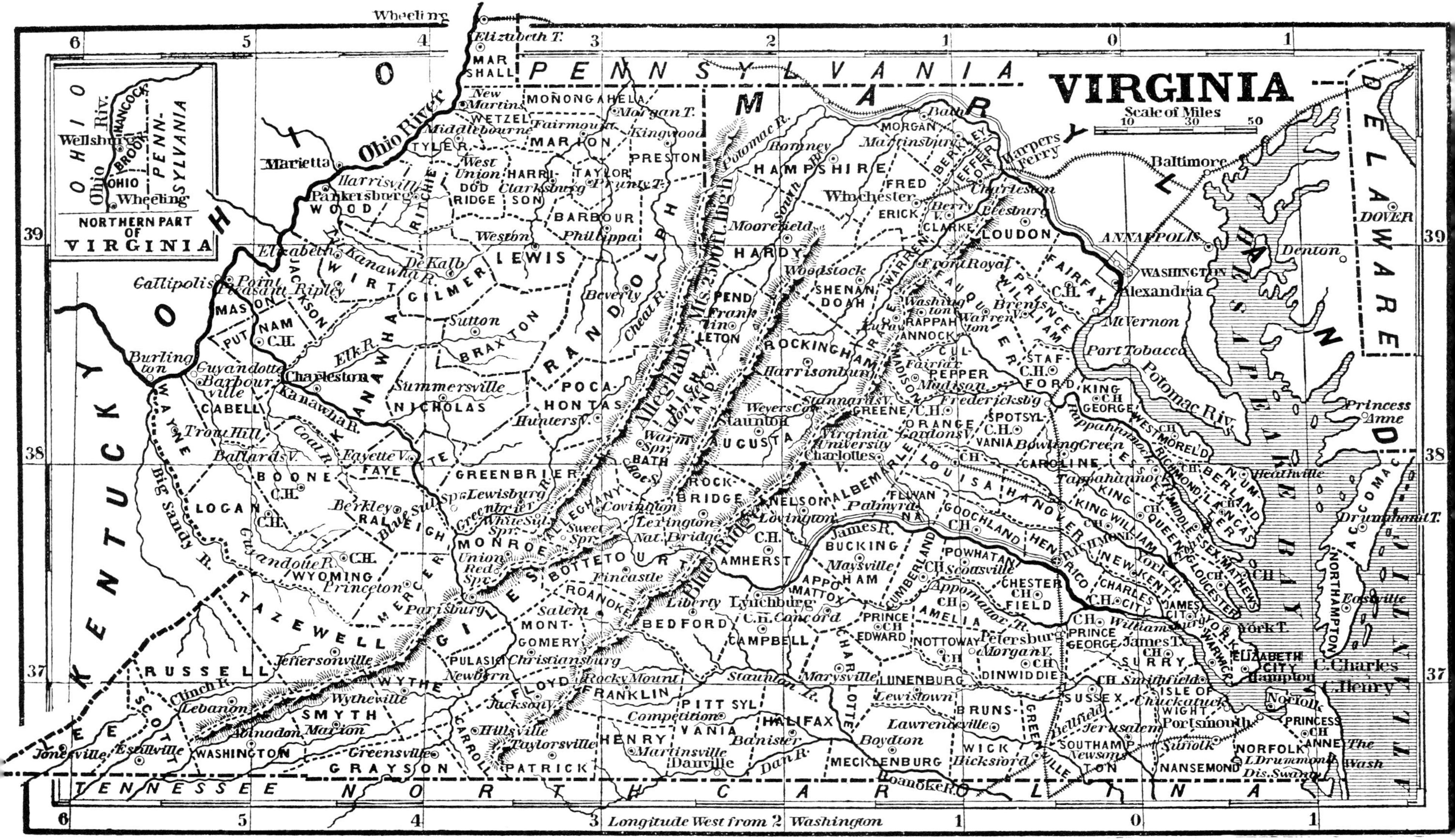

VIRGINIA

Scale of Miles
10 30 50

Longitude West from Washington

Reproduced from an original 1853 map by Jonathan Sheppard Books, Albany, NY 12220.

VIRGINIA-1853

BRIEF BIOGRAPHY

The Civil War history of the Virginias has been of special interest to Jack Dickinson for the past 30 years. He has authored three other books on the Civil War: *Records of the 16th Regiment Virginia Cavalry,* CSA; *Confederate Soldiers of Western Virginia;* and *8th Virginia Cavalry.* Jack is one of the founders and charter members of Camp Garnett, Sons of Confederate Veterans. He is also a Certified Genealogist and has lectured before various groups and published several articles on genealogical topics. He holds a B.A. degree from Marshall University in Huntington, W.Va. Jack is employed by IBM Corp. in Huntington as an advisory systems engineer.